Great Glass
in
American
Architecture

Great Glass
in American
Architecture

DECORATIVE WINDOWS
AND DOORS BEFORE 1920

H. WEBER WILSON

E. P. DUTTON   NEW YORK

This book is dedicated to
Diane Rill Wilson
a successful woman, a terrific mom,
and the Lady of my life.

Illustration on page i: This leaded silhouette of a fisherboy and his dog was made in the 1930s for the front door of the house where the author grew up in Seattle, Washington.

Illustration on pages ii-iii: American glass realism, c. 1890. The branches of this heavily laden tree sprout leaves and fruit cut from richly colored and textured cathedral glass. The background is subtly shaded to suggest the sky on a hot summer day.

Illustration on page v: Enlargement of one of the stained-glass doors shown on the front cover of this book. This three-part composition typifies the era when American glass focused on romantic concepts and natural motifs. The pearly opalescent glass of the background intensifies the sunlight, and it also reflects moonlight on the water of the pond. Among the delightful details in this stunning creation are a bird, an owl, a frog, and toadstools, which were hand painted and fired.

Book design by Marilyn Rey

First published, 1986, in the United States by E. P. Dutton. / All rights reserved under International and Pan-American Copyright Conventions. / No part of this book may be reproduced or transmitted in any form or by any means, electronic or mechanical, including photocopy, recording, or any storage and retrieval system now known or to be invented, without permission in writing from the publishers, except by a reviewer who wishes to quote brief passages in connection with a review written for inclusion in a magazine, newspaper, or broadcast. / Published simultaneously in Canada by Fitzhenry & Whiteside Limited, Toronto. / W / Published in the United States by E. P. Dutton, a division of New American Library, 2 Park Avenue, New York, N. Y. 10016. / Printed and bound by Dai Nippon Printing Co., Ltd., Tokyo, Japan. / Library of Congress Catalog Card Number: 85-70842. / ISBN: 0-525-24318-6 (cloth); ISBN: 0-525-48176-1 (DP).
10 9 8 7 6 5 4 3 2 1 First Edition

CONTENTS

ACKNOWLEDGMENTS

Research for this book was supported by a Design Project Fellowship from the National Endowment for the Arts in Washington, D.C., a Federal Agency.

The author would like to render thanks to the following for their interest and help, which have made this book possible:

The American Life Foundation and its director John Crosby Freeman for publishing their invaluable collection of American architectural material and for permitting many of the illustrations to be reproduced in this book.

Doug Cooper and Keith Curry, who understand American decorative windows, and are as pleased to sell as they are to buy.

Walter Folger, the photographer for many of the color plates in this book, who was always ready to shoot just one more window.

Lili Lihn in New York, a publicist par excellence and a valued mentor.

Sean and Janet McNalley for sharing their knowledge of American stained glass and their fine collection of windows.

Cyril I. Nelson, the editor for this book, for his help along the way.

. . . and to B and A for their very special contribution.

CHAPTER ONE

An American Legacy of Color and Light

America has a treasury of decorative windows which represents the most diverse artistry imaginable. In towns and cities, in buildings both public and private, our country has a wealth of antique architectural glass which exists in every imaginable shape, size, color, and texture. In fact, the variety, the quality, and the different construction techniques represent a historical and artistic phenomenon.

Significantly, the best of this delightful, brilliant glasswork is a manifestation of the uninhibited, eclectic American spirit of the last half of the nineteenth century. That was a period when an abundance of money, manpower, and materials resulted in spectacular national growth. There was also tremendous individual success throughout all cultural levels.

These social achievements were the result of an economic revolution which introduced the modern age. Industry and commerce were reshaped to meet the demands of an expanding nation in which needs and popular taste began changing at an accelerating rate. Unheard-of concepts such as the elevator and electricity would be introduced, and improvements in communications and transportation would allow the United States to develop at a rate, and with a spirit of cooperation, which was without precedent.

Here was America moving into high gear, and the ultimate source of this generative power—for the successes as well as the mistakes—was the freedom which inspired its citizens to dedicate themselves to dreams of the future. Time and time again they saw these dreams fulfilled within their own lifetime.

Culturally, one of the most important proofs of this success is found in our nineteenth-century architecture, in particular the surviving residential and commercial buildings found throughout America today. These buildings have often been criticized as symbols of an elaborate and illogical era. But generations of everyday people have continued to live and work in these stimulating, comfortable spaces and have come to recognize the generally fine workmanship, and the continual delights of nineteenth-century decorative detail. Paramount among the fascinating details found in such buildings is the glasswork filling innumerable windows, doors, skylights, entry canopies, and even fireplace screens.

Decorative windows were, of course, not a new idea, but beginning in the second quarter of the nineteenth century, colored glass was literally rediscovered, and in America especially, adopted as a new material. Consequently, it was used here in more diverse and imaginative ways than ever before—the most creative result being the development and evolution of what is called American stained glass.

The effects of colored light have always been a source of fascination: perhaps from the sparkle of its intensified energy; perhaps from the way it elevates a viewer outward and back toward the source of its mysterious force. For America in the pre–Civil War decades, this was a brand-new experience. By the end of the century, glass artisans in this country had taken both the manufacture of the material and the creation of decorative windows into new realms of beauty.

1. This lettered transom window, c. 1890, has richly colored and strongly textured glass cut to enhance internal grain and shading. Numerous jewels help refract the light and the orange ribbon provides a pleasing contrast. Acid-etched Gothic lettering, Renaissance-inspired foliage, and a stylized Greek shell are blended into a distinctively American decorative style.

2. Oriel windows sprouted from all types of buildings in the late 1800s. Often they featured transom lights filled with highly decorative glass.

3. The builder of this stained-glass, oak, and brownstone entryway probably had never seen a classic ruin, but there is nonetheless a strong feeling for antiquity in this 1890s townhouse.

4. This stained-glass entrance canopy, c. 1895, shows how decorative glass was used effectively in institutional as well as residential and ecclesiastical architecture.

5. This brass and stained-glass fire screen and the sculptured terra-cotta fireplace were both created in the late 1880s. They were recently transposed to a more contemporary setting.

The key factor here was that colored glass became an affordable commodity rather than an expensive luxury, and production and creative use were, in turn, stimulated by a new emphasis on architectural decoration. The American experience became both national and prolific. It was inspired but not restrained by history, and was nurtured in a social and economic atmosphere which emphasized freedom of choice, and unlimited personal expression. The result was that by the last quarter of the century American glass artists had embarked upon one of the great creative episodes in history.

By the 1880s, American buildings had become as individualistic as the men and women responsible for their design and construction, and American glass artisans were simultaneously developing many types of decorative windows to complement the new architectural styles. Besides the well-known stained and leaded glass, other processes such as etching, beveling, wheel engraving, and a number of quite unorthodox techniques found great popular acceptance in the United States. Additionally, a number of wholly new glass varieties and window styles were invented by our glass artisans; so many, in fact, that it is probable that they will never be completely catalogued.

Fortunately, there are enough antique decorative windows still extant to show the breadth and depth of American glass in American architecture, and the surviving examples of unusual styles and special techniques provide the inspiration for us to keep searching for more. Indeed, for those who look at windows, as well as look *through* them, it is an aesthetic delight that so many great examples remain for us to enjoy.

Some Contradictions and Confusions

The subject of "Victorian stained glass in American architecture" is actually a historical malapropism. Taken singularly or together, the terms *Victorian* and *stained glass* have much more to do with the history of Great Britain than with the history of the United States. Neither term adequately describes the development of American architecture in general or American decorative windows in particular.

Queen Victoria reigned for most of the nineteenth century with a presence and an influence which engraved her name as strongly in America's culture as in the culture of Great Britain. She was crowned in 1837 at the age of eighteen, and at her death in 1901 she had become synonymous with one of the great epochs in Western history. It was the period which saw Europe, led by England, colonize the world. It was also the period which saw the greening of America.

But the monumental changes which occured during the sixty-four years of Victoria's reign cannot be put into perspective by a single adjective. Each decade of the nineteenth century saw the present move rapidly from even the immediate past, and for both America and Europe, the changing perspectives became kaleidoscopic. In fact, there were so many strong opinions about architecture that the resulting debate became known as "the Battle of the Styles."

Just a partial list of styles which influenced American building during the 1800s include the Greek Revival, the Shingle style, the Arts and Crafts Movement, Neo-Classicism, and the beginnings of Modernism. None of these is thought of as being specifically Victorian, and each added its own personality to the period. This, in turn, has strongly affected the history and reputation of American decorative windows, which continues to be involved in a twentieth-century religious dispute that has effectively obscured the tremendous accomplishments of our earlier, secular glass artists. In addition to the cultural/architectural confusions, there is the added problem that the term *stained glass* is very misleading.

The chief difficulty is that there is really no stain in stained glass. Glass color is obtained during the initial stages of production, depending upon the chemicals used in the molten mix, and glass artists of every era—whether Medieval, Victorian, or Modern—have had their palette limited by the quality and variety of glass produced during each period. In the eleventh and twelfth centuries, production methods were crude, and color selection limited. Then, during the thirteenth century it was discovered that a solution of silver nitrate, when applied as a clear solution on glass and fired at about 1100°, would become a light yellow to deep orange color. During the firing, this "silver stain" became permanently fused with the surface of the glass, and this vitrified, golden color was used to represent hair, halos, and other images where a bright, radiating glow was desired. Thus, even though the art of colored, mosaic windows had already been established for several centuries, the success of this particular decorative technique came to represent the whole concept of stained glass.

Most European languages describe colored-glass windows with some variation of the Latin word *vitrearum*, which can also be translated as *window pane*. In English, however, we speak not only of *stained glass*, but also of *painted glass*, for historically, the application of dark, vitreous oxides has been as artistically important as the selection and cutting of the glass, and the formation of the leadlines which make up the basic mosaic pattern. Thus traditional European stained glass stresses a mosaic of crisply colored glass that uses a coating of fired paint to control the quantity and intensity of light.

European stained glass has evolved through several periods of contrasting styles, the most uninteresting era being the seventeenth, eighteenth, and early nineteenth centuries. During these "Impoverished Years" glass artists focused on brightly colored enamel paints and applied them to larger and larger sheets of clear glass, much as a

The Apple of Discord

6. An acid-etched whimsy, c. 1900.

7. A late nineteenth-century beveled side-light with a design that anticipates the Art Deco style of thirty years later.

8. In the 1880s, businessmen enjoyed decoration at work as well as at home. This interior transom window is set in an oak frame that complements the curves of the brilliant-cut design.

9. The so-called mercury mosaics of the late 1880s are one of America's most fascinating innovations in decorative glass.

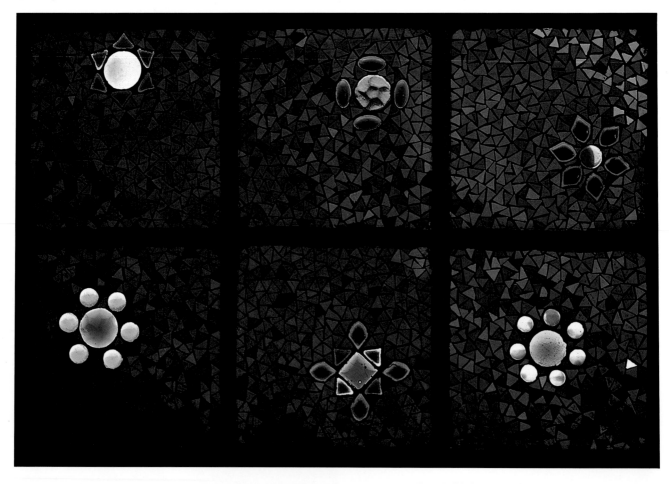

painter would work on a blank canvas. Such work was rarely successful, and it was during this period that the medieval techniques were discontinued and interest in the art reached its historical nadir. Significantly, this also meant that there was basically no transfer of a decorative glass tradition to the architectural heritage forming in the New World.

In fact, it was not until the second quarter of the nineteenth century that the American glass industry became established. By then, America was not inclined to look backward toward ancient—and foreign—precedents. Rather, this country approached the medium of glass with a fresh vitality. The result is that for America, the sustaining architectural application of decorative windows has been secular, with artists steadily eliminating the use of paint and stain and generating maximum creativity from the glass itself.

At the same time that American glass artists were reinventing their medium, American architects were mixing and matching structural and decorative components with a verve and enthusiasm that produced buildings which were as often unusual as they were successful. Thus emerged a dynamic, eclectic spirit: a romantic yet confident outlook that encouraged a multi-faceted, people-oriented environment. It was a spirit that sustained a large segment of American building up through the first decade of the twentieth century.

It was within eclectic architecture that decorative windows found their most comfortable and complimentary surroundings. And in response to these nontraditional buildings glass artists developed and perfected a whole spectrum of new decorative window treatments. Unfortunately, American stained-glass history has thus far been written by the traditionalists with the result that most of the public—and many scholars as well—still haven't been able to fit "American stained glass" into a logical historical context.

As a final indication of the difficult time that "American stained glass" has had in adjusting its image, the Stained Glass Association of America, in 1962, ran a survey of its members to ". . . redefine the term stained glass . . . ," and among the several professional opinions offered were:

Stained glass is an assemblage of various pieces of different colors and shapes of glass held together with either strips of metal or by different kinds of compounds. Some color pigments may be burned onto the glass to create details of a pre-determined design.

Architectural, translucent, color integrated glass panels . . .

. . . avoid mention of a specific medium, such as glass, staining, leading, conchoidal, et al., and use a phrase such as "decorative panels," which even avoids the window limitation . . .[1]

10. This illustration from Edward Hazen's *Panorama or Professions and Trades*, 1837, shows that in the second quarter of the nineteenth century the standard window was still rectangular and multipaned.

Two decades after this attempt to find a more workable definition of a thousand-year-old art form, we have still not moved far from square one. But a better understanding is growing, especially through the nineteenth-century secular windows which continue to impact upon our daily lives. Ironically, they are mostly anonymous art, but just like the windows of the medieval years, they have survived with grandeur into a wholly new time.

Painters, Glaziers, and Anonymous Art

If one were to enumerate the reasons why American decorative windows are so fascinating, one of the chief reasons would be that the majority were created by artists who will forever remain unknown. Tiffany Studios, which is by far the best-known name in American stained glass, produced hundreds of windows which were never recorded as to their place and date of installation. Indeed, when windows of the best-known artists receive such haphazard attention, it's easy to see why a beveled entryway in Richmond, Virginia, or a jeweled transom in St. Paul, Minnesota, will probably never have its originating studio, let alone the actual creator, identified. Even a brief survey of American decorative glass shows that the number of quality examples easily moves into seven figures, but so far, the basic sources and styles of this profuse display of public art are yet to be identified.

An enlightening description of America's early window artists is to be found in Edward Hazen's book, *The Panorama or Professions and Trades or Every Man's Book*, published in Philadelphia in 1837. In his preface, the author notes that ". . . many individuals escape their appropriate calling . . . ," and proceeds to describe in detail every occupation, from the "Dyer and Calico Printer" to the "Coppersmith and Buttonmaker." Significantly, there is no

11. A twentieth-century religious window executed with strong Medieval influence. Note that the details and shading are effected with fired-glass paints and silver stain. Note also the reliance on strong, primary colors.

12. American church windows of the 1880s eliminated paint and stain and took advantage of a new palette of glass that featured strong textures and variegated colors. Such windows also emphasized decorative rather than symbolic themes.

13. *Modern Architectural Designs and Details*, published by William Comstock in 1881, featured some houses with decorative glazing.

mention of stained glass, but there is a thorough description of the "Painter and Glazier," from which we can begin to understand how the tradition of American decorative-window production began.

As advice to would-be painters, Hazen spends much time discussing the preparations of various materials used in house paints, adds several tips on how to obtain and keep a good business reputation, and warns against unscrupulous suppliers as well. Along the way, he mentions that the painter/glazier was also the man who made the commercial signs which ". . . relates to forming letters, and sometimes ornamental and significant figures . . ." [2] Further on, he refers to " . . . the house and sign painter. . . ," [3] and then provides details on specific aspects of *ornamental painting*:

> Ornamental painting embraces the execution of friezes and other decorative parts of architecture on walls and ceiling. The ornaments are drawn in outline . . . then painted and shaded, to give the proper effect. Some embellishments of this kind are executed in gold leaf, in the same manner with gold letters, on signs. This kind of work is called *gilding in oil* . . . [4]

After a detailed description of the gilding process, Hazen discusses the work of the glazier, and begins by saying:

> Glazing, as practiced in this country, consists chiefly of setting panes of glass in window-sashes. In the performance of their operations, the glazier first fits the panes to the sash,

by cutting away, if necessary, a part of the latter with a chisel . . . [5]

and then notes that ". . . plain glazing is so simple, that no person need serve an apprenticeship to learn it. . ." [6]

Hazen adds a pertinent observation that:

> . . . there are but few who confine their attention to this business exclusively. It is commonly connected with some other of greater difficulty, such as that of the carpenter and joiner, or house and sign painter. . . [7]

It is from this association between the painter, glazier, sign maker, and housewright that the American stained-glass trade evolved. Traditionally, house painters were responsible for the repair and reglazing of windows because when glass was expensive, and few people had experience working with it, window repair was often put off until the building was repainted. In the course of his work, the painter would scrape the windows, observing any problems with the glass, and it therefore fell to him to learn how to cut and trim the panes, and how to set, or "glaze," them into the sash, and sometimes, into the cames of leaded lights. Eventually, the painter or "decorator" became the person who would accumulate a supply of glass and learn new techniques in handling both plain and fancy windows.

Even today there are small, local painting or decorating businesses which, as a regular part of their service, repair all manner of windows. Such operations are of the "old-time" category, but they often keep a small garage or an all-but-forgotten storeroom containing an amazing supply of old glass, lead cames, and all the other materials necessary for the creation and repair of decorative windows.

The demand and production of decorative windows expanded and contracted in direct relationship to the fortunes of local housing and commercial building opportunities. The decorator/glazier would be part of this economy, and success for the small operator would hinge upon being able to provide a selection of creative services at irregular intervals. When buildings were going up, and decorative windows were ordered, the decorator would order glass and often hire skilled, itinerant artisans to complete the work. Evidence of this is to be seen in neighborhoods across the country, where in several blocks of buildings decorative windows with very similar characteristics can be found. That such windows came from the same studio is usually easily determined by the similarities of glass, jewels, and designs. A few blocks away, there is often another group of buildings where similar decorative glass can be identified.

Up through the early part of the twentieth century, there was a tremendous quantity of outstanding glasswork being produced in America with much of the very best work coming out of local workshops and going into local homes and commercial buildings. At the same time, requests for dramatic, graphic, commercial signs caused the decorator/glass shops to develop such techniques as sand blasting, beveling, gilding, and imaginative, typographical windows.

Glass artisans have traditionally been reluctant to share their ideas, but in the nineteenth century, with new decorative windows being installed everywhere, a particularly attractive design, or imaginative solution to a problem in fenestration, became part of the public domain as soon as the building was completed. Thus, enthusiastic public acceptance would cause the production of other windows with similar effects of line, color, and architectural emphasis. As the neighborhoods and cities expanded, the quality and variety of decorative windows observable from the street became like a permanent, public pattern book.

Glass artists were often hired as temporary help, finding lots of opportunity when building activity was strong, but also finding themselves out of work when the projects were completed. Such economic uncertainty kept the creative juices flowing, no doubt, and also dovetailed with the wanderlust which is a characteristic of many creative people, even today. These skilled craftsmen would move across the country, providing the creative skills necessary to augment local operations, and would bring with them the ideas and successful decorative applications from other projects.

This combination of local and itinerant talent, operating within the deadlines of the building industry, meant that the records of most projects were usually just temporary documents, which became submerged and eliminated as other piles of papers took their place. Cartoons for decorative windows are particularly expendable, and it was as easy to draw up new and slightly modified designs as it was to save and recopy old patterns. Thus the real record of the early glass artists is, therefore, in the windows which still exist, and not in the generally diluted designs of the large commercial producers who could afford to market their products by means of well-printed catalogues. Such companies, by the early twentieth century, had pretty much taken over the production of American decorative windows, but were forced steadily to reduce the quality of their designs and the quality of the glass, which eventually reflected on the reputation of the industry.

Decorative Windows in American Homes

In 1878, Henry Hudson Holly (who shall be heard from again) commented on how residential stained glass could be effectively used in homes of the period:

> It would be proper to use . . . stained glass . . . in windows over a staircase landing, and indeed in all sashes above the height of the eye . . . This idea is borrowed from the Gothic, and . . . we do not hesitate to accept it as being extremely beautiful, and capable of the most artistic treatment . . . Designs of fruit, game, convivial scenes, and texts of good cheer furnish appropriate decorations.

> Staircase windows particularly offer an opportunity for stained glass when they are placed above a landing, thereby coming into a central position between the two stories, they serve the double purpose of lighting both . . . When introduced in a proper hall, I mean, one serving more as a room than a passage, stained glass is appropriate, even if not admitted to any other part of the house. In the panels of the hall door, also . . . stained glass would be appropriate, as its obscure effects would serve the purpose of preventing passersby from seeing in . . . Upon the fan lights it could also be well applied . . . [8]

These citations provide a good idea of the many uses which were suggested for stained glass, and a survey of actual buildings shows that all these ideas, plus many others were used by builders and homeowners of the late 1800s. Undoubtedly, the most popular use of stained glass was as a transom light, either above a door or a window. Transom windows are usually rectangular, but they can also be found as squares, semicircles, and chord shapes.

Sometimes it seems as if every front door in America has a transom light above it. Often, the design of the glass incorporates the street number of the building. Often, too, one finds a name or even a message written above the entry, especially if it is a commercial building, or a church.

14. This engaging portrait window shows definite English influence, but the colors and composition are typical of American work of the 1870s.

15. This 1890s rowhouse features a multistory oriel window with thirteen transoms, two of which were installed upside down.

16. This six-part, Neo-Classical entryway exemplifies the changes that occurred in American residential stained glass around the turn of the century. High-quality glass is used throughout, and the floral details are finely wrought, but the simple geometric backgrounds, and the uninspired designs of the sidelight transoms show that economic pressures and conservative tastes were causing major reductions in stained-glass creativity.

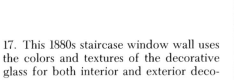

17. This 1880s staircase window wall uses the colors and textures of the decorative glass for both interior and exterior decoration.

18, 19. Plate 54 of *New Cottage Homes*, published by Palliser, Palliser & Co. in 1887, showed a stained-glass window built into a chimney.

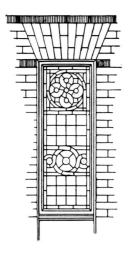

It was also popular to use decorative glass around the front door, forming integrated entryway sets. These multi-window combinations most frequently include a pair of vertical sidelights framing the door with a transom window across the top. Often, more than three panels are used, as when the transom window is itself divided into sections. By the 1880s, the fanciest entryway sets also had a matching door panel, and many large houses featured an additional interior entryway of wholly different glasswork.

The use of small stained-glass transoms above larger clear windows was a pleasant way to include decoration and colored light within a room while simultaneously maintaining clear window glass at eye level. Frequently, window transoms are found in multiples, across the tops of oriel or bay windows. At other times, single, large transoms were used as major stained-glass compositions topping a series of smaller windows underneath. Transom windows, generally, are set permanently into a wall opening, but the movable sashes of many double-hung windows were also filled with decorative glass. Here, one can find a variation to fit every option: stained glass in only the upper sash, in both sashes, or in the same sash of several adjacent windows. If both sashes have stained glass, there can be two identical designs, two separate designs, or a single, overlapping design, where the border connects the perimeter of the combined sashes.

Architects of one hundred years ago were generally very careful where they used stained glass, and knew that strong, bright colors and complex designs could overpower a room, or prevent a person from visually escaping to the outdoors. That is one reason why clear or obscured glass was used in abundance, and why, for all their bulk, late nineteenth-century homes are still refreshingly light and airy. The result is that many of the finest examples of residential stained glass are set where they are seen only as one moves from one area of the building to another. The main hall with its fancy entryway is a good example; and the stairway area was probably the second most popular place to install elaborate decorative glass.

The spaciousness of Victorian architecture, with its large rooms and large windows, provides a special sense of satisfaction when moving about, and the main staircase in such homes is a key traffic area. Usually, the area is wide, and includes at least one turn, or landing area, and it is in this spot that one finds the most spectacular windows of all.

Just like transom windows, stairway windows come in all sizes, shapes, and combinations. Sometimes they are singular, sometimes double hung. Frequently they appear as sets, either as a group of decorative panels moving along with the rise of the staircase, or in the prime examples, as entire sections of a wall, composed of numerous individual windows, but glazed to form a single, spectacular design or scene. Sometimes landing sets included figures, usually in classical dress, and the inclusion of a peacock was also popular. Throughout America there are thousands of exquisite stairway windows, either figural, scenic, or floral, whose creators will never be known, but whose artistry continues to bring inspiration to generations of delighted homeowners.

In most houses of the period the second floor contained the bedrooms and the bath, and although stained glass is sometimes found in bedrooms, it is usually because the windows are part of the fenestration on the front of the building. Other rooms facing the street were enclosed by towers or turrets, or had oriel windows attached, and it is in these spaces that decorative glass is more likely to be found.

Stained glass for the bathroom was as important as stained glass for the parlor, however, and some great decorative glass is found in both areas. Mention should also

20. You don't need a book in the bathroom when you have this patchwork window to study. Note the great ruby crackle jewel, typical of American glass originality of the 1880s.

21. In the mid-1890s, this pair of exquisite roundheaded windows were created simply to illuminate a short passageway between two large commercial buildings.

be made of the many smaller but highly complex windows, found in the oddest nooks and crannies, which are actually seen better from the exterior than from the inside of the house. These windows can be spotted in many unusual shapes, and often, when one goes into the building to see the glass with backlight, it turns out that the window was set in a closet, lost in a desolate corner, or even completely walled over. Finding such windows, however, is part of what makes American windows, and American eclectic architecture, so much fun.

Normally, one finds stained-glass windows in the first two stories of a house, although many windows, with designs formed with wooden mullions, are often seen in gable ends, or protruding dormer windows. Commercial buildings, however, often were built to include store fronts at street level and apartments above, and thus there are numerous examples of high quality stained glass along the skylines of America's Main Streets.

Many old buildings also have decorative glass as interior as well as exterior embellishment. The most popular interior application is door panels, and there are often two entryways: one opening onto the street, and a second separating the vestibule from the main hall. Here one often finds etched, wheel-cut, or beveled panels in place of leaded mosaics. Many times, the interior entryway contains much more complex work than that on the exterior.

Within the homes and commercial buildings of the late nineteenth century, decorative glass was set in door panels, particularly in sliding, or "pocket" doors, and in office doors which required strong, but obscured light. It is also common to find built-in furniture such as cupboards, or china closets with leaded glass doors or panels, and some homes also feature large, ornate stained-glass panels in interior hallways, even though there is little backlighting available. It is unusual to find interior transoms filled with decorative glass, except when they are part of the entryway into a special room, such as the library. However, it is fairly common to find stained-glass panels set into openings which were built right through the brickwork of a chimney.

Altogether, the designers and decorators of nineteenth-century eclectic buildings felt free to install decorative glass just about anywhere that light, color, and imaginative design could add a touch of class. The success of this fresh and open approach to windows and window fill was for many decades discounted by twentieth-century builders, but a century later, American architecture again finds itself being inspired by the glass art of the past.

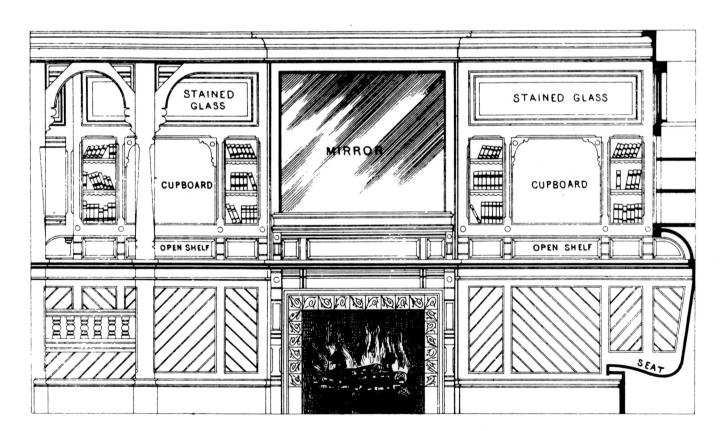

22. Comstock, 1881, Plate 56. Stained glass is recommended, but the choice of designs is left up to those who will build the house.

CHAPTER TWO

Romantic Architecture and Colored Glass

The United States reached the 1820s believing that a national building style was not only desirable, but very possible. Then, like a cultural leavening agent, Greek Revival architecture inspired symbolic, unadorned, temple-fronted buildings all across the expanding national territory. From Maine to the Mississippi, there was a belief that through the Greek mode, commonly shared building forms would provide the built environment wherein the growing political and social problems could be sagely and successfully resolved.

The United States could still think of itself as a small country where commercial and agrarian interests held a relatively even balance, and the continuation of Classical building ideals was therefore logical and expected. But the Greek, along with the last splashes of Roman formality, were to prove no match for the surge of commercial, political, and social power which, when released, would send the country spinning through the last half of the nineteenth century and right on into the twentieth. It was time for new and freshly focused styles, and as noted by Alan Gowens, the influence of eighteenth-century Classicism had run its course well before mid-century:

. . . by the 1840's, the whole rational of the [Classical] revivals had collapsed . . . originally conceived as a symbol of political liberty, they had been extended in so many diverse and contradictory ways as to become virtually meaningless as a symbol. Freedom of business from government interference, and freedom of government to regulate business; freedom of religion and freedom from religion; freedom from slaves, and freedom to keep slaves; the rights of free labor, and the privileges of free capital . . . the wonder is . . . that the Greek and Roman Revivals dominated American architecture as long as they did.[1]

Unquestionably, the old order was changing and a close look at the architecture of the second quarter of the nineteenth century shows two brand-new building styles going up alongside the tall columns and bright white walls of interpretive Greek. One style is known as "Italianate," and the other is called "Gothic," and together they represent the spearhead of a movement which, when it began, was labeled "Romantic" or "Picturesque," and fifty years later had blossomed into the numerous variations now broadly known as "Eclectic." Along the way, social, commercial,

23, 24, 25, 26. Lyndhurst, the National Trust property in Tarrytown, New York, is a superb example of American Gothic Revival architecture. It was begun in 1838 by Alexander Jackson Davis and enlarged by him two decades later. Most of the original windows were composed of broadly cut, leaded quarries, and some of these, such as in the stair tower, were later enhanced with cut-glass fillets. The circular window was devised and installed in 1864. It is hinged in the middle and includes blue and yellow flashed glass. The chord-shaped window has stenciled designs that are typical of mid-century American decorative glass.

27 (*above:* Providence, built 1828); 28 (*below:* Boston, c. 1862). By the 1860s, the austere forms of the Greek Revival had given way to an eclectic spirit.

and architectural changes would occur in quantum leaps, creating an age of so many styles, movements, and opinions that even a century later it is hard to view it all within a rational perspective.

Culturally, the big change was occurring in population growth, from both the indigenous birthrate and the stead-ily increasing immigration. New people brought new ideas and new cultural ties, with the result that France and England no longer monopolized America's perception of foreign thought and style. At the same time, the swelling population began to affect urban centers, creating a whole new series of social problems from basic life support to sewage disposal. This in turn sparked the concept of planned, suburban housing developments, so that by the 1860s it was possible to be a city worker but a country dweller. As an indication of the monumental changes which were occurring, there is the very pertinent, although historically minute, detail that in the 1840s, it was necessary for someone to invent the lawn mower.

The basic reason for all this change was wealth: genera-ted, accumulated, and dispersed in untold quantities by unheard-of numbers of people. There seemed no limit to the economic spiral of supply and demand, and although there were recessions along with the boom times, con-tinuing improvements in production, distribution, and marketing never slacked. It was a time that saw the forma-tion of that most American of concepts: consumerism.

These great economic changes caused hardship for many, but for just as many others it provided the opportunity to prosper as a national citizen, a local resi-dent, and especially as an individual. The concept of being "American" also represented stability, and there developed an increasing interest in what had always been the corner-stone of our culture: the family home. A very substantial house became a very achievable goal for thousands of families that a generation or two before could never have hoped to attain such a symbol of success. Industry, meanwhile, was making the unimaginable commonplace, causing dramatic shifts throughout architecture as each social and economic segment of society was required to find separate solutions to separate problems. In the 1830s, one would have seen houses, banks, and churches, all in the Greek Revival style. A decade or two later, this cohesiveness was dissolving as dissimilar factors began affecting dif-ferent building types.

The prime example of this was seen in the development of commercial property, where the intensified use of limited urban land left no choice but to build up instead of out. The result was a structural revolution which allowed buildings to rise higher—and faster—than ever before. Solutions to other needs, such as spanning the great areas of railway terminals and waterways, the building of mas-sive mills and manufacturing plants, the enclosure of whole city blocks for retail space and financial transactions, resulted in a landscape which rapidly filled up with what are best described as commercial cathedrals. The creation of such structures not only commanded tremendous energy and resources, but when completed, these build-ings dramatically symbolized a larger-than-life testimony to the supra-American influence of business and profit.

29 (*above:* Philadelphia, c. 1854); 30 (*below:* Hartford, c. 1884). By 1880, America's urban centers were filled with richly decorated architecture that was testimony to modern ideas and private wealth. These commercial cathedrals also exerted a powerful influence on homebuilding.

At the more personal yet very profitable level of individual housing, other precedent-setting changes occurred. During the 1840s, the introduction of the balloon frame, standardized lumber, and machine-made nails virtually reinvented the process of house construction. Next, the new housing industry produced and promoted very decorative elements as well as designs, so it became not only popular, but downright easy for great numbers of people to think in terms of building their very own dream house. Wood continued to be the principal home-building material, but brick, stone, terra-cotta, and cast iron also found application on buildings which continued to grow texturally richer. Among all the materials which found a wider, more decorative use, it was probably glass which made the most dramatic and most long-lasting impact.

The New Material: Glass

America's trade relations had been severely strained by the War for Independence and the War of 1812, but the positive effects of those conflicts resulted in fresh impetus being given to the national development of several key industries. Glass manufacture was one of the most important and was helped by immigrants who understood the manufacturing process and could take advantage of the great resources and potential market here. One of the earliest areas to manufacture glass was "out west," along the Monongahela River near Pittsburgh. There was additional activity in New England, New Jersey, and Maryland, where a few glass houses enjoyed relative success before 1800. Within the next three decades, however, more than a dozen glass producers emerged in New York State alone.[2]

The initial products had been bottles, window glass, and hand-blown glassware, all of which were available in limited quality, quantity, and variety until the second quarter of the 1800s. By the 1830s, however, American ingenuity had begun to take advantage of the many utilitarian characteristics of glass, and well before mid-century, glass items had become established as readily available marvels of a New Age. Domestically, glass was tried at least once for everything from water pipes to keys for pianofortes, but its shift into everyday usage is best exemplified by the mass production of inexpensive pressed-pattern glassware which began in the late 1820s and is still an important industry today. We, of course, take for granted an abundant supply of inexpensive plates, cups, and glasses, but in the 1840s, the availability of such a product represented a significant shift of social expectations.

By the 1840s, also, except perhaps for the meanest houses of the frontier, window glass was found everywhere. The most popular residential window style continued to be multipaned, mullioned sash, although the longer, narrower windows of the new Italianate architecture were beginning to attract attention. The most dramatic shift—and dis-

31, 32. This advertisement from E. C. Hussey's *Home Building*, 1876, indicates the broad appeal of ornamental glass. The house represents American "Steamboat Gothic" at its finest.

play—of fenestration occurred in the context of the big, sometimes huge, commercial buildings which required "commercial size" windows. The need for more light, more display, and more ventilation was being met by new building techniques which by the 1850s included large cast-iron arches to support the increased heights. The areas between these large openings were ideal for architectural embellishment, and the fenestration of these big, new commercial structures set the concept of decorative windows firmly in front of an interested and attentive public.

Residentially, the Greek Revival lingered on past midcentury, but the "newness" of the expanding urban centers and the "sameness" of the rural areas grew more evident. New houses going up everywhere began to feature win-

dows with larger panes of glass and more dramatically displayed fenestration. American glass established itself as a material that would continue to diversify, and it was probably inevitable that the next important application would be the incorporation of colored glass in windows.

Glass tinted green or blue or yellow had always been available, mostly created from the impurities found in the basic ingredients, but there was little American interest in taking advantage of this creative factor until well into the second quarter of the nineteenth century. Then, it is interesting that one of the first uses of colored glass to generate several historical mentions was the popularity of decorative steamboat windows. These windows were composed of geometric, mullioned panes, and river travel around midcentury, as described by Mark Twain, must have been considered a magical flight, with:

> curving patterns of filigree work, touched up with gilding . . . big chandeliers every little way. . . lovely rainbow-light falling everywhere from the colored glazing of the skylights; the whole . . . a bewildering and soul satisfying spectacle.[3]

These flamboyant rivercraft also left a lasting impression, with their decorative woodwork both above- and below-decks, and the potential for such an expressive building

33. America adopted the Gothic Revival style with studious dignity, as seen at Lyndhurst, and also with unabashed revelry, as shown by this building.

34. Greek Revival buildings did not feature colored glass, but the ornamental motifs of that style later found great favor with American window artists. The most popular element was probably the palmette or shell form, as featured in this oval window of the 1880s. In the center is a hinged ventilator panel.

style was soon transposed into the very American "Steamboat Gothic" house. Other applications of colored glass turn up in these fanciful houses, such as wheel-cut designs, sometimes on flashed glass. Such work was mostly used for corner pieces or border fillets, and as an indication of the increasing popularity of colored glass, a variety known as "Pittsburg ruby" was being advertised as early as the 1840s.[4]

During this time, Europe continued to focus on painted glass, although ecclesiastical historians consider the early nineteenth century as a period when traditional stained glass was pitifully close to extinction. There are records of American companies displaying "stained and painted windows" as early as the 1830s, with these "pictures on glass" probably being produced with enamels. There are also records of American churches importing "stained glass" as early as the 1820s, but these too must have been painted panels, all of which have apparently been lost.[5] However, records of the glass companies and architectural pattern books show that by the 1850s the use of colored glass had become an effective, practical, and modern option for stretching the inelastic perimeters of Classical architecture into the exciting potential of the unfolding century. Already, fiery, opaline milk glass had become popular for household articles, a distinct portent of the spectacularly colored and textured windows which would shortly follow.

Antebellum Windows

The shift toward Romantic architecture in the second quarter of the nineteenth century introduced much more than just a new style of building; it introduced a new cul-

35. Gothic Revival houses too often spoke of starched collars and stilted conversation. Such a style might be good for churches, but it was not the way many workingmen wanted to end their day.

tural perception of man and his environment. Classicism had represented man's ability to create a world above, and independent of, the hostilities of nature. Romantic builders, on the other hand, saw the natural world as a pure and softly changing organic force where people could retreat and lose the frustrations of the workaday world.

This new appreciation of nature was first expressed through the Gothic Revival which had been simmering in England since the last half of the eighteenth century and by the 1840s had come to be regarded as the British national style. Many Britons had always preferred their own ancient ruins to those of Greece and Rome; a cultural perception that some consider a golden thread and others refer to as a brackish stream. Regardless, the introduction of Victorian Gothic into the United States instigated a major architectural turnabout.

This new building style was significantly more dramatic than the shift out of Pilgrim century "Wrenaissance" building and into Georgian forms. That had been calm, aristocratic, and refined; a change that reflected *class* as well as classicism. This Gothic revival, on the other hand, was for many a cult of the bizarre, emanating from the minds of English eccentrics and manifested in what was often considered outrageous construction. Early on there was Fonthill Abbey, an incredibly expensive pile built for William Beckford, a rather loosely wrapped English scion to industrial wealth, who proclaimed: ". . . I grow rich and mean to build towers . . ."[6] This he did to the height of nearly 150 feet which later, to the surprise of no one, collapsed not once but twice. In the United States, there were such Gothic enthusiasts as the goodpenny Bishop Doane of New Jersey who shipped himself to New York in a wooden crate.[7] And across the country, a whole passel of simple, visionary types spontaneously encased or encrusted their otherwise staid houses within veritable wombs of sawn-wood ornament.

Such wacky interpretations of the style were, unfortunately, very much a reflection of the erudite neo-Gothic philosophers who themselves are remembered as much for their odd behavior as for their reactionary views. The best known of these are John Ruskin and Augustus Welby Northmore Pugin, both of whom wrote extensively and influentially on the need to switch from what they perceived as the "pagan" forms of Greece and Rome, back to the "Christian" architecture of the medieval centuries. As influential as their philosophy became, however, Ruskin has been described as ". . . with the possible exception of Pugin [the] single theoretician in architectural history who has done more to deflect it into unproductive detours and cul-de-sacs . . . ,"[8] and A. W. N. Pugin is recalled as a man who was ". . . forever proclaiming that Gothic architecture and sailboating were the only true joys in life, finally going mad and falling out of his sailboat to drown . . ."[9]

If this also sounds like the opening salvos in the Battle of

36. Italianate houses expressed family life and casual country living. It was a style of Romantic architecture that remained popular for several decades.

the Styles, it is, to the extent that such strong statements delineate the widely differing opinions on architecture (and social development in general) which have competed for acceptance since the decades just prior to the Civil War. The Gothic Revival, with its idiosyncrasies and oddball personalities, was only the first style to emerge as an alternative to the Classical norm which was crumbling before the pressures of a complex industrial society. America, especially, was looking ahead, not behind, and as we sought the opportunity to display both personal and national success, this country gravitated to other styles which could be just as individualistic, but which were much more in tune with our own historical perspective.

The most important of these "Gothic alternatives" was the "Italianate" style, which eventually became almost as popular as the Greek mode it succeeded. In America, the Italianate style found a very comfortable middle ground between the Classic and the Medieval forms, where architectural tastemakers produced a fresh style which nonetheless contained many familiar decorative elements such as columns, porches, pediments, and balustrades. Perhaps even more important, the Italianate style was both noncontroversial and sophisticated, a relaxed and flexible alternative to the upright and uptight Gothicism.

Italianate styles were also synonymous with villas, a term that brings on thoughts of peaceful country living. Gothicism, too, had stressed natural surroundings, but those high-pitched gables with ornamented bargeboards, and pointed arch windows with quarried, mullioned sash evoked images of brambles rather than cultivated shrubbery, and primeval surroundings rather than broad expanses of green, velvety lawn. The Italian style was simply more *picturesque,* a quality about which there arose expansive discussion, and which would lead directly onto the forthcoming popularity of Eclecticism.

The new building styles began in the Northeast, but quickly spread into every state and territory, aided greatly by the availability of pattern books. Pattern books had influenced architecture and architects as far back as Palladio, but up until the mid-1800s, the material had emphasized specifications, often discussed in very dry, technical terms. Such books were written more for the builders than the building owners, but as a surge of home-owning swept across America, the pattern book publishers began to emphasize the "ambiance" of structural choice, leaving the details to professional carpenters and masons who were expected to have the skills required for actual construction.

Best known among the antebellum architect/illustrators was the combination of Alexander Jackson Davis and Andrew Jackson Downing who offered books with titles like *The Architecture of Country Houses Including Designs for Cottages, Farm Houses, and the Best Modes of Warming and Ventilating.*[10] The emphasis here was homes, occupied by people, with examples and explanations of every up-to-date article from "bed cupboards" to "speaking tubes." Architects found that success depended on flexibility, and so most pattern books promoted popular trends and offered examples of several types of buildings in several different modes.

The subject of windows is given adequate coverage in these early pattern books, although the specifics of window fill are generally left up to the imagination of the viewer. There is enough mention of decorative glass to provide evidence of when and in what forms it began to find application in domestic architecture, and considering that these books are reports of what had been happening as much as encouragement for new concepts, various glass treatments can be considered established about the time they rate a mention.

Some of the earliest illustrations of nineteenth-century leaded window fill occur in *An Encyclopaedia of Cottage, Farm, and Villa Architecture,* by John C. Loudon, a self-educated Scotsman who published extensively, but unprofitably, in the 1830s. Loudon's book illustrates two interiors with windows glazed with simple leaded quarries, one of which also has sheer curtains. In a section specifically about curtains, the windows are all standard

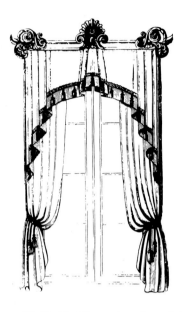

37, 38, 39. Illustrations from John C. Loudon's *An Encyclopedia of Cottage, Farm and Villa Architecture*, 1833. Some quarrywork is suggested but highly decorative windows are a long way off.

double-hung sash, which was the predominant style in the United States until at least the 1840s.

One of the contemporary American books that shows the architectural details of this period is Hazen's *Panorama of Professions and Trades,* where period window styles can be seen in the environments of the occupations discussed. Nowhere is there a discussion of decorative glass, but in the section on "The Architect," Hazen discusses Classical, especially Greek design, mentions both the Egyptian and Gothic revivals, and even illustrates a "Chinese Pagoda." In his discussion of the Gothic, Hazen explains that:

> The Goths...were not the inventors of the style of architecture which bears their name. The term was first applied with the view to stigmatize the edifices of the middle ages; in the construction of which, the purity of the antique models had not been regarded...

...The Gothic style is peculiarly and strongly marked. Its principles seem to have originated in the imitation of groves and bowers, under which the Druid priests had been accustomed to perform their sacred rites...[11]

Hazen also notes that "...in the erection of edifices at the present day, the Grecian and Gothic styles are chiefly employed..."[12] which indicates the extent to which the Romantic styles were beginning to supplant the traditional Classic. The numerous windows which appear in the backgrounds of his illustrations reiterate the gradual adaptation of decorative fenestration and provide a fascinating glimpse of how the people, and the built environment of 1830s America, actually appeared.

The title page, for example, shows "The Author," pensively sitting in an armchair, behind which is a round-headed window filled with an intricate pattern of mullioned panes. There is also a bookcase in this room, which has quarried doors. Further into the book, Hazen shows "The Druggist and Apothecary" in his shop, the entrance transom to which is a decorative light featuring a curvaceous design which evokes the next generation of mosaic glass. Comparing these windows with the illustration of "The Clergyman," however, shows just how little the concept of "stained glass" had progressed, for here, behind the preacher, are tall windows filled only with large expanses of small, rectangular panes.

It was during the 1830s that colored glass became generally available, and its potential use in secular windows became recognized. The "academic" medium of stained glass was still confined primarily to painting enamel pictures, although there was an increasing interest in both Europe and America to work with something other than clear glass and geometric shapes. In 1836, an obscure stained-glass artist apparently provided windows for a church in Newburgh, New York,[13] and other American companies were apparently making painted glass windows at about this time. Unfortunately, none seem to have survived.

Up until the early 1840s, figural church windows were almost all imported but in 1843, the first religious, mosaic stained glass that is recognized as American made was created by William Bolton for Christ Church, in Pelham, New York. One year later, two major American stained-glass projects were begun for Trinity Church in Lower Manhattan, and for the Church of the Holy Trinity, Brooklyn Heights. Windows for Trinity Church were made by Abner Stephenson, working in a shed near the construction site. Windows for the Church of the Holy Trinity were created by William Bolton, assisted by his brother John. The interest generated by these two major projects certainly inspired other congregations to use stained glass in new construction, and gradually to replace the old, clear windows as well.

40, 41, 42. Illustrations from Hazen, 1837. Windows in the Author's study and in the Apothecary shop indicate a move toward decorative glass, but the Clergyman preaches in front of basic, roundheaded, multipaned lights.

Thus, American ecclesiastical mosaic windows initially sought to imitate traditional painted symbolic styles; but simultaneously, if not before the Boltons and Stephenson, secular decorative window makers had discovered the pleasures of designs that emphasized both leadlines and the unadulterated color of the glass. The earliest secular,

colored-glass windows have yet to be identified, although the Philadelphia firm of Euston and Weer were listed as "painters" in the city directories beginning in 1839, and were eventually recommended to A. J. Downing as experienced residential window designers.[14] Downing himself mentions stained glass in *Cottage Residences,* published in 1842, and by the early 1850s, other pattern books were suggesting a variety of applications for both "stained" and "figured" glass.

In 1850, A. J. Downing published *Country Houses,* in which an "Interior in a Simple Gothic Style" is shown fully furnished. At the far end a large, multisectioned window is shown, glazed with quarries, probably set in wood, and which also features a decorative border. About this room Downing remarks that:

> The bay window opening at the end of the parlor…shows the Tudor arch, and the side window, a square-headed window, with the style recognized by the introduction of the arch in the woodwork of the architrave. To our own feeling there is more domesticity in square-headed windows…[15]

A few pages later, Downing shows another room, at the end of which is a four-part leaded window, in which diamond-shaped quarries have been further decorated with simple designs. Discussion in the text is limited to the spaciousness of the room, an indication, perhaps, that decorated windows were by this time well enough established as not to require specific mention.

Downing also refers to the "Elizabethan" or "Renaissance" style, the former being the English term, the latter, the French. Regarding this up-and-coming mode, Downing says:

> …Elizabethan or Renaissance Style…in a philosophical point of view…often violates all rules of art, and indulges in all manner of caprice. Mere architects and pedantic judges have accordingly condemned it in all ages. Viewed, however, as a style addressed to the feelings, and capable of wonderfully varied expression, from the most grotesque and whimsical to the boldly picturesque and curiously beautiful, we see much in the style to admire, especially for domestic architecture.[16]

Here is another barrage in the Battle of the Styles, and though not presented with antagonism it indicates the difference between Downing and John Ruskin, for example, both of whom were vying for the attention and support of basically the same public. Downing illustrates numerous examples of the new Renaissance-style furniture, and it is interesting to see how design elements such as the paneled doors, or carved mirror frames and wardrobe pediments, contain the shapes and configurations which would later be transposed into decorative window forms.[17] It is evident that the Gothic style was struggling to retain domestic influence in the United States, and in his section

43, 44, 45. Illustrations from *The Architecture of Country Houses; Including Designs for Cottages, Farm House, and the Best Modes of Warming and Ventilating,* by Andrew Jackson Downing, 1850. These windows feature painted quarries and colored border fillets and provide a new look for American homes.

on "Furniture in the Gothic Style," Downing remarks that:

> ...The radical objection to Gothic furniture, as generally seen, is that it is too elaborately gothic—with the same high pointed arches, crockets and carving usually seen in the front of some cathedral...Hence, in many of the finest Gothic mansions, abroad, Elizabethan or Flemish furniture has long been used in preference...as combining the picturesque and the domestic far more successfully...
>
> There has been little attempt made at adapting furniture to the more simple Gothic of our villas and country houses...Yet we are confident this may be done in...style...adapted to and expressive of our modern domestic life.
>
> In the meantime, we give a few examples of Gothic furniture...hoping for something better in the way of design at no distant time.[18]

As part of these illustrations, Downing quite calmly plagiarizes designs published in Loudon's *Encyclopaedia,* of 1833, probably because it was easier simply to copy something previously prepared, but also because the Gothic style was not well established here, and Downing's heart was not into locating the better class of furniture which he claims he would like to see.[19]

Four years after Downing's *Country Houses* appeared, Oliver P. Smith published *The Domestic Architect,* but titled, in part, as *Original Designs for Rural and Ornamental Cottages...of the Grecian and Cottage Style.* In his preface, Smith says that:

> ...the prevailing style of country building, in the United States, is exceedingly faulty...[and] to correct this prevailing fault...to adorn every village and town with beautiful residences and elegant villas—is a desideratum of high importance...[20]

46. This transitional window dates from the early 1870s and shows how American glass artists began to move away from the painted, Gothic mode. Windows like this showcased the color and grain of the glass, and introduced the three-dimensional energy of jewels and other decorative inserts.

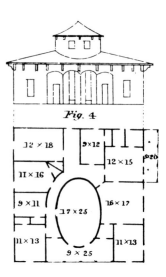

Fig. 4

47, 48. Plate XLI (above, left) from *The Domestic Architect* by Oliver P. Smith, 1854, shows a Gothic Revival cottage typical of the period. Plate XXVI (above, right) features a house where "…the roof of the cupola…is lighted with stained glass…"

Within his discussion of the various styles of his time, Smith talks at length about the Egyptian, although mostly as historical reference, and also discusses the Gothic, although his comments are primarily borrowed from Hazen. His real interest is the Cottage style, which for him is "…a modern style of domestic Architecture…without the cumbersome complications which mark the Gothic when used for ecclesiastical purposes [and which] harmonize admirably with the picturesque rural scenery of this country."[21] The illustrations he provides are generally unpretentious homes which emphasize rectangular massing and symmetrical fenestration, embellished with sharp gables, porches, and sawn wood ornaments cut in Gothic forms.

Smith's buildings mostly incorporate only clear, classically styled mullioned sash, although one design does show additional transom lights in the dining room and parlor, and the accompanying note mentions that this is "…a cottage of but one story, the parlor situated nearly in the centre…The ceiling to the parlor is in the roof of the cupola, and lighted with stained glass…"[22]

In 1859, the United States Capitol was under construc-

tion, and stained-glass ceilings were installed in both the House and Senate chambers. These great expanses of decorative glass were made by the firm of J. & G. H. Gibson Company of Philadelphia, and are indicative of the American movement toward decorative architecture and decorative glass. Indeed, well before the Civil War, glass had become accepted as a colorful, creative material that could be used in "multifarious" ways.

As the antebellum era drew to a close, the medium of secular glass art was firmly establishing its own creative space. The influence of the English Gothic Revival had certainly been significant but in too many ways it had come across the Atlantic as a romantic wish to turn back the clock. Such reactionary ideas were tailor-made to self-destruct against the economically oriented, style-conscious juggernaut which was American culture at midcentury. Artists in the United States were viewing glass as a new and profoundly creative medium, and thus the development of American windows would continue to respect the principles of ancient ideas but their creative exuberence would never stay within any confining, historical bounds.

CHAPTER THREE

Decorative Windows for a Decorative Age

When the Civil War ended in 1865, America was very much a new country again. Just as had happened after the struggle for independence, the nation found itself on a wide and open road, where natural and cultural resources abounded, and where there seemed to be room and opportunity for everyone. This time, however, there was no identity crisis to be resolved, no foreign domination to be purged, and only pockets of hostile land left to explore and absorb. America was established, and although our internal struggles had resulted in the despair of families at war, the underlying currents of growth had never really slowed, so that the end of hostilities also signaled a new era of American enterprise.

This era would showcase mechanical, commercial, and political power of unparalleled intensity, making it possible for ambitious people to reach their goals. This might mean controlling a railroad, operating the local hardware store, or simply owning a large, comfortable house away from the turbid bluster of the city. A good place in life was eminently possible, and without pretentious scholarship insisting upon new directions, Americans became more

and more individualistic, neither fearful of the future nor weighted down by the past.

This became especially apparent in architecture, where engineers and builders sought to create satisfactory space for residential, commercial, ecclesiastical, and institutional occupants. Each of these categories had different needs, and each was anxious to take advantage of the new products, materials, and services directed specifically toward them. The challenges were tremendous, but so were the potential rewards, and the result was a built environment designed to both complement and contain the new culture which was emerging out of the lusty, laissez-faire capitalism.

Creative divergence between architecture and decorative windows begins with the buildings of the 1860s and 1870s, a period often referred to as "High Victorian," but which is still early in the evolution of architectural colored glass. This was a time when some new styles were created and some old styles embellished; and while the use of decorative windows became more widespread, the most creative decades of secular stained glass were yet to come.

49. Around 1890 an asymmetrical style of window emerged to complement the vigorous, Eclectic building styles that prevailed throughout America. This fine example was salvaged from a demolished house, and it displays "free classicism" at its grandest. Greek shell and key motifs rest above a brace of Renaissance volutes that enclose an Aesthetic sunrise. Bringing together these elements is an indigenous American network of jewels and beveled inserts, set with just enough irregularity to create a powerful visual tension.

It was the beginning of the great age of Eclectic home-building, however, with a widening choice of building styles and decorative components available everywhere. Exteriors began to emphasize multiplicity of form, aided by the introduction of central heating which allowed buildings to be designed as spacious and sprawling as funds allowed.

The steadily increasing mechanization of building materials production had little initial effect upon decorative windows, which continued to be handcrafted and therefore considered a local product. Architects and pattern-book publishers increasingly suggested the use of colored and figured glass, but because the ultimate choice was up to the building owner, actual incorporation of decorative glass was very much at the slower end of the overall trend toward increasingly ornate building styles. By the 1880s, this hesitancy had been completely overcome, so that builders themselves were installing decorative windows along with the gingerbread facades, mirrored mantelpieces,and heavily turned and carved newel posts. Increased demand generated a greater and more diverse supply, and the great decades of American glass began.

Ironically, even though interest in all varieties of decorative windows remained strong until the early part of the twentieth century, it was during this same time that several other critical forces began building an inertia which would eventually overwhelm the accomplishments of America's nineteenth-century glass art. Most important was the dramatic shift in building style away from Eclecticism, and toward a "new" Classicism, an "old" Colonialism, or a variety of unheralded "Modern" styles. Significantly, all these movements were very evident in the 1880s—at exactly the time when American glass art was ascending—and in combination, steadily obliterated the sort of fenestration in which decorative glass could be effectively sustained.

Concomitantly, the increasing popularity of highly decorative glass activated a Gresham's-law effect where mass-produced, lower-quality glass began to drive out the high-quality, custom-made work. This happened over many years, but in the end, even though decorative windows were available everywhere, few people cared.

Contributing to this unraveling of American glass artistry were the owners of the stained-glass studios who could not find the patience to cooperate until near-demise was inevitable. By the 1920s, the surviving American artisans had all but disowned the accomplishments of the nineteenth century, and our own glass historians carried forward an animosity which effectively blacked out one of America's most prolific artistic periods.

The story of American decorative windows therefore becomes an unfortunate combination of enlightened creative evolution and debilitating economic struggle. The legacy that survives is still trying to fit itself into the history of both art and architecture.

Light for the Brown Decades

Post–Civil War building saw the continuation—and enrichment—of both the Gothic and Italianate. It also saw the beginning of a long association with contemporary French taste, and the introduction of the very American "Stick style." Each of these architectural varieties incorporated decorative glass on a selective basis, and each contributed to the total impetus which edged American glasswork onto the fast track of creative development.

High Gothic, or Ruskinian Gothic as it is sometimes called, set the tone of the period with multicolored facades, rising up to steep gables and crested towers. Polychrome effects were created by using different colors of brick and stone, and textural contrasts were achieved with materials such as sculpted terra-cotta and tiles. John Ruskin continued to write and proclaim his English philosophy, but the reality was that in the United States his ideas were steadily transmogrified by the influence of other Gothic notions. This bigger, stronger, Gothic style was most evident in public building, and established decorated architecture as a dominant form for the upcoming decades.

Many of the commercial Gothic buildings featured leaded windows glazed in soft, cathedral tints. Sometimes the windows also had special medallion centers which featured a highly detailed design. Transom windows were set above many front-facing lights, and probably because they were given a deep setback, they were most often glazed with clear glass set in vertical, double-hung sash.

If one wished to commission especially decorative glass for a high Gothic residence, it would likely have been an enameled scene, or perhaps a geometric design stenciled onto leaded quarries of clear or cathedral glass. Roundels and pressed-glass inserts were known at this time, and these special decorative inserts were also occasionally used. The result was that even though Gothic architecture was soon to lose all but its ecclesiastical supporters in America, this "olde world" style encouraged the early American glass artists to begin the creative transformation of their medium.

The initial alternative to High Gothic was High Italianate, which didn't change dramatically from its forms of the 1840s except to expand when built as a single-family dwelling, and to contract like an accordion when incorporated into a string of city rowhouses. It was as popular for commercial architecture as for residential buildings, and although it did not feature decorative glass in the front windows, the imaginative treatment of the window surrounds became a great and continuing inspiration for more decorative window fill.

Italianate houses are known for the curvaceous brackets

50, 51. New York's Jefferson Market Courthouse (now a library) was designed in the early 1870s and represents the High Gothic spirit in American commercial architecture. The decorative windows reflect what was prevailing English taste, although from the outside (shown at the left) the American movement toward more secular designs can be seen. From the inside it is also evident that there was a continued emphasis on fired paint and silver stain.

52. This "building-block" window dates from the 1870s and has a pattern stenciled and fired on cathedral glass. The stenciled border fillets are cut from red flashed glass.

53. The wide leads used in this roundel flower panel indicate that it dates from the 1870s. Also note the medallion silhouettes and the primitive cathedral glass.

54. An illustration of a mansard roof from *Architecture and Rural Art* by George E. Woodward, 1868. Note the oriel window (at the right), which he asserts "...has proved a desirable feature, especially to the ladies..."

found under their eaves, and for the quantities of applied decoration, either as layers of moldings, hoods for windows and doors, or specially formed details taken from the Romans and Greeks. Many of these houses feature cut-glass entryways and have special treatment of the windows in the stairway landing as well. The best-quality interiors were filled with black walnut and white marble, and this sleek combination was more and more reflected in fancier windows for the parlor, the hall, and the bath. Where cut or leaded glass was not yet in style, front doors often had their street number gilded onto polished plate, sometimes as part of an extensive design which might include sandblasting and enamel painting as well.

In San Francisco, Italianate houses are famous for their tall, multiple-light "bay" windows which add greatly to the total ambiance of the brightly painted and highly ornamented streetscape. The Italianate style could be made efficient for city office space, and comfortable for city living, and it became a favorite of the immigrant capitalists who soon made up an important segment of the sector of successful, middle-class American entrepreneurs. The Italianate style stayed on until near the end of the century, so that today one finds veritable country villas seemingly lost and forgotten in the midst of modern urbanity.

The 1860s also saw the introduction of the "mansard" roof to America, a French idea which gained immediate notice. This roof is unmistakably different, with a "broken" appearance which creates two separate slopes, and often features round or oval windows up at the skyline. This roof originated with the French architect François Mansart and was first used on the château at Blois in the 1630s. In the late nineteenth century, the mansard roof became a hallmark of the "Second Empire" style, which became synonymous with French prestige throughout the world. In America, a style of extremely ornate stained glass evolved out of the increasing interest in French decoration, which, for this country, offered a whole menu of fresh architectural choices.

The Second Empire style was quite romantic, with towers and pavilions and an arresting display of exotically shaped and situated windows. There was an aristocratic air about these places, whether commercial or residential, and such ready-built grandeur had an obvious appeal to the increasing numbers of nouveau riche. Like the other styles of the 1860s and 1870s, there was not much colored glass used, and little decorative window fill facing the street. But the vibrant fenestration provided much visual enjoyment, especially with the dormer windows and the ornate window surrounds of the upper stories and roof.

It is likely that such creative window shapes and lush window surrounds were among the first architectural openings to receive the highly ornate, colored mosaics which began to appear in the late 1870s. The Gothic was too ancient and religious-looking, and the Italianate too "countrified," but the regal bearing of the Second Empire

55. Plate XVIII in Palliser's *Model Homes*, 1878, is an example of the American Stick style. There is Queen Anne glazing in the transom windows.

56. The mansard-shaped window dates from the 1880s and reflects the popularity of the mansard roof, which had become popular during the previous decade.

57. This is an especially decorative Queen Anne sash, c. 1885. There is lots of English influence in the painted panels, but the complete composition is American.

would very comfortably display a highly colorful, multi-piece entryway set surrounding massive, polished, hardwood doors. Certainly, when American residential stained glass reached its mature years of tightly leaded, heavily jeweled, intricately detailed designs, houses of the French taste received some of the highest-grade decorative glass.

Architectural history sometimes seems like a "Builders' Olympics," and as might be expected, the post–Civil War decades had an American entry right beside the English, Italian, and French. In many ways the quietest of group, the Stick style rests calmly and often unobtrusively among the more florid European styles of the same period. It is a style invariably built from wood, and along with sharp gables and extensive porches, this construction is distinguished by articulated "stickwork" superimposed over the clapboard siding.

This appliqué of wood over wood is meant to stress the "truthful" use of the material, and is applied in a pattern representative of the basic framing. There was much concern around midcentury about the philosophy of "honest" buildings, and it is interesting to note that the first American effort at interpreting these ideals was quite truthful indeed.

The Stick style is important in the evolution of American decorative windows because it was our first indigenous architecture to display colored glass in a light, airy, and

58. A "suburban villa" from *Country Seats* by Henry Hudson Holly, 1863. "…The grand feature of this house, next to the hall, is, undoubtedly, the stairway, which occupies a large space at the left, and is well lighted by a stained glass window…"

unpretentious manner. Builders of Gothic villas—and Gothic castles—had been incorporating decorative windows for several decades, but set in a context of brooding stone walls, domineering gables, and a rather uptight style of living. The Stick style, on the other hand, gave Americans an architecture which suited very well the new way of life evolving here: self-confident, expectant, and designed for warm family living.

Stick-style houses most often used Queen Anne sash in the upper half of double-hung windows, and from the outset it was apparent that colored panes could be as easily glazed as panes of clear glass. The most basic pattern was formed with small rectangular panes surrounding a large center pane, but the variations on this theme are innumerable. Queen Anne sash was also sometimes embellished with such additional detail as cut-glass corner medallions, or panes of sandblasted "lace glass." Sometimes pressed-glass tiles were inserted, and sometimes small, leaded mosaic panels were also incorporated.

This use of Queen Anne sash in a large segment of American residential building created a broad, new awareness of the possibilities of colored glass in architecture. It also introduced the concept of using highly decorative glass in the upper sash of a window while leaving the lower sash open for light and visual contact with the outside.

In the 1860s and early 1870s, American Eclectic buildings and decorative glass in particular were immeasurably aided by the new generation of architectural pattern books which began to fill mailboxes all across the country. The continuing improvements in printing meant that books could be larger, more detailed, and less expensive, and with a national mail service providing rapid distribution, families in every state could share the excitement of studying floor plans, elevations, and specific decorative details. There were dozens of titles and thousands of illustrations by both competent and incompetent designers, and while the objective of many pattern books was to sell homes as well as illustrate them, the most enduring aspect of these publications is that by taking a chronological sampling, one can follow the development of residential architecture along a fascinating historical vista.

For example, Henry Hudson Holly became nationally known with the publication of *Holly's Country Seats* in 1863, a book which he noted "…was fully prepared for the press some two years since…when the War for the Union broke out, and…the author, therefore, thought proper to postpone the publication until affairs should be in a more settled state…"[1]

The book itself is comprised of thirty-four "Designs," each one including a sketch of a dwelling and a page or two of discussion covering everything from "where a gate lodge is appropriate" to "finials and ridge ornaments of practical utility." There is little mention of decorative

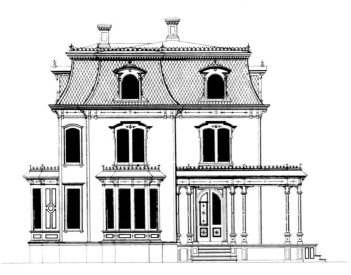

59. A typical illustration from A. J. Bicknell's *Village Builder*, 1872. Note the mansard roof and detailed decoration, but blank window fill.

glass, but in Design No. 19, which was a Gothic villa apparently built in New Haven, the "description of the plan" includes mention that: "... The grand feature of this house, next to the hall, is, undoubtedly, the stairway, which occupies a large space at the left, and is well lighted by a stained glass window."[2]

Close to the end of the decade, in 1868, George Everston Woodward published *Architecture and Rural Art No. II*, which was his second book in two years. He introduced this new publication with the comment that:

There is a growing appreciation for improved styles of building which is being recognized throughout all the better settled portions of our country...

In No. I of this series a large number of designs were given for low-priced cottages, farm-houses, etc.... This number is devoted more particularly to a class of houses contemplating a more liberal expenditure, and introducing examples of the French or Mansard roof, which is attracting attention from all...[3]

And further along, when discussing windows, he suggests that:

... Windows to be of the size shown; all sash to be hung with weights and provided with fastenings; sash to be 1½ inches thick, and glazed with the best quality French glass.

Front doors to be glazed as shown, with French glass. Bay and parlor windows to be paneled to the floor; all others finished on sills.[4]

These references to French roofs and French glass indicate how that nation's influence was coming on, and also points up the appeal of "imported" ideas and materials. The country was becoming more and more affluent, a fact which was recognized by both indigenous and foreign manufacturers, and also by local contractors who saw every building going up as an economic opportunity to which they could supply the latest in materials, services, and fashionable goods. In response to this demand, and in hopes of generating even more sales, the pattern books of the 1870s began to feature large-scale drawings of specific decorative elements along with the usual illustrations of elevations and floor plans.

This trend was made evident in A. J. Bicknell's *Village Builder*, published in 1872, which provided precise drawings for just about every house part from gable ends to stairway spindles.[5] The *Village Builder* is also noteworthy for being a collection of "... original work, comprising the designs of fifteen leading architects, representing the New England, Middle, Western and South-Western States..."[6] Some of these men were or later became well known, and the designers of five extant state capitols are represented. Other designs given credence by Bicknell's book can be most courteously described as "interesting," with features such as porches and basements shown without access, and in one instance, the end of a kitchen is given over to a matched pair of bedrooms, each 7½ feet square.[7]

Nonetheless, Bicknell provided an important link in the evolutionary chain of American residential building, for he not only illustrated complete houses and individual details, but he also provided many pages of actual contracts and building specifications, plus an important section of illustrated advertisements at the end of the supplementary section. Decorative windows are nowhere specifically mentioned, although a study of the designs shows many windows and doors where decorative glass could be expected. Plate 2, which is a "Design for a French

60. A typical house illustrated in Bicknell's *Detail, Cottage and Constructive Architecture*, 1873.

61. This ornamental quarry from Christopher Dresser's *Principles of Decorative Design*, 1875, shows some strong suggestions of Art Nouveau.

Cottage," notes, under the specifications for "Painting and Glazing," that:

> ...All of the sashes are to be glazed with the best German glass, all to be well bedded, bradded and back puttied. The front doors are to be glazed with ground glass of such pattern as may be selected. All other glass panel doors are to have plain ground glass.[8]

Bicknell published another pattern book in 1873, entitled *Detail, Cottage and Constructive Architecture* which dispensed with editorial comment, and went right to the basic issue: providing as many illustrations of as many variations of building components as possible.[9] The title page to this book is indicative of the actual contents, and Bicknell provided his readers with a virtual smorgasbord of architectural embellishments. Windows are shown in dozens of shapes and sizes, but there is no indication of decorative window fill, with the spaces between the mullions staring back with about as much expression as Little Orphan Annie's eyes. This is intriguing, because it is apparent that the application of residential decorative glass had established its popularity by this time, yet it is not featured in this pattern book (or others, either) which are all but overflowing with every sort of architectural ornament. The mention of decorative door panels also indicates that ornamental glasswork was well known, but in regard to windows, it is apparent that most of the work was being done at the local level, and additionally, the concept of artistic window styles was still not yet an expected part of American building.

In 1875 *Principles of Decorative Design*, by Christopher Dresser, appeared. Subtitled "Truth-Beauty-Power," it discussed all aspects of ornament and design in response to

62. Dresser's concept of "...what stained glass may advantageously be..." This window design of the late 1870s could easily command attention in a stained-glass gallery of the 1980s.

what had become, in both Europe and America, a very decorative age. The ideas and especially the illustrations of Dresser's book are decidedly English, but his basic philosophy that not only is decoration a valid artistic expression, but that "...the beautiful has a commercial or money value..."[10] was certainly the sort of encouraging talk which would have been enthusiastically absorbed in this country. Dresser's book included a chapter on "stained glass," in

63. American Eclectic buildings, such as those erected for the Centennial Exposition in 1876, represented an international amalgamation that confounded historians and critics.

ancient glass-painting traditions were continuing as a strong influence in England throughout Victorian times. Most of the glasswork is composed of decorated quarries, certainly meant to be hand-done, but also easily produced with stencils. The actual components of the designs are fascinating, however, as they clearly relate to, although are well in advance of, the Arts and Crafts, Art Nouveau, and Art Deco movements. In particular, the largest illustration, which Dresser describes as "…my view of what stained glass may advantageously be…"[13] would fit into an exhibit of the most modern glass of the 1980s, especially if it were executed with lead cames rather than simply painted.

The Aesthetic ideas of Christopher Dresser were to find considerable acceptance in American decorative building, but his specific concepts of stained-glass designs were rarely adapted here. The application of paint to enhance the decoration of glass was very selectively employed in American residential windows, primarily because the palette of our glass artists was being steadily enriched with an astounding choice of color, texture, and opacity. Nonetheless, Dresser's encouraging discussions of decorative-glass application were undoubtedly influential, and as the great Centennial celebration of 1876 brought the world to the doorstep of America, his ideas were one of many inspirations which set up a spectacular decorative climax to the century's closing years.

The Best Years of American Residential Stained Glass

The appeal of Eclectic building had gained tremendous momentum by the late 1870s, resulting in significant change in housing styles. Decorative windows had evolved

which he provided a good look at the medium as it was in England in the 1870s. Similar ideas were being simultaneously applied to American buildings, and Dresser's comments provide a good description of the position of secular stained glass just before the great creative surge of the 1880s. In part, Dresser said:

> …If a window commands a lovely view let it, if possible, be formed of but few sheets…of plate-glass;…but if the window commands only a mass of bricks and mortar inartistically arranged, let it, if possible, be formed of coloured glass having beauty of design manifested by the arrangement of its parts.[11]

Dresser did not believe in windows treated as pictures "…with parts treated in light and shade…" but it is apparent from his illustrations that his concept of "stained glass" was irrevocably entwined with "painted glass," for he speaks of creating "…the distinction of part from part…by the strong black outline which bounds the parts and furnishes the drawing of the picture…" Additionally, he felt that "…it is not necessary…that much strong colour be used; tints of creamy yellow, pale amber, light tints of blue, blue-grey, olive, russet, and other sombre or delicate hues, if enlived with small portions of ruby or other full colours, produce the most charming effects…"[12]

The stained-glass illustrations in *Principles of Decorative Design* are significant in that they clearly show how the

64. The frontispiece of Palliser's *New Cottage Homes and Details*, 1877, illustrates the multiplaned roofline that so enticed American Eclectic architects. Decorative windows were used profusely in houses similar to this example.

65. This illustration from Bruce J. Talbert's *Examples of Ancient & Modern Furniture Metalwork Tapestries Decorations Etc.*, 1877, was actually exhibited at the Royal Academy in 1871. Note the style and placement of the decorative windows.

also, and by the middle of the following decade had moved from the geometry of quarries and ancient-looking painted medallions into wholly new and profoundly creative designs. Utilizing a veritable rainbow of sensuously textured glasses, emphasizing complex, tightly leaded compositions, and incorporating a luscious assortment of jewels and other special inserts, American glass artists fashioned ornamental configurations and naturalistic scenes with a profound brilliance and realism.

The transition took several years, and a number of events combined to cause dramatic shifts in both architectural direction and decorative-glass concepts. Most significant was the Centennial Exposition of 1876, the grand and nationwide celebration which not only showcased the United States as one of the world's great nations, but even more importantly, brought the cultures of the world into the lives of thousands of Americans who had never seen a foreign country. The results were dramatic and direct: by

66, 67. American Queen Anne architecture is best known for prominent gables, dominant towers, sawn-wood decoration, and Eclectic window fill. Such an eclectic or "free classic" spirit is evident in this 1890s residence that features a pointed Gothic window filled with Renaissance motifs, several fleur-de-lis, a center medallion, and jeweled swags.

the mid-1880s Americans had enthusiastically absorbed, in part or in parcel, the habits, philosophies, and fashions of an international community that was sharing improved communications, nonchalant travel, and educational exchange.

Architecturally, a key result of the Centennial was the inspiration of a new style of homebuilding now known as Queen Anne. Not surprisingly, these nineteenth-century American buildings had little resemblance to English architecture of the Queen Anne period in the early 1700s. In fact, the first American Queen Anne house is credited to Henry Hobson Richardson, who built a sprawling seaside "snuggery" in 1874 that featured exposed timber framing and a roof that appeared to be cut and folded in order to cover the eccentric arrangement of spaces below. Significantly, Richardson chose wooden shingles to sheathe the upper walls, and from this there shortly evolved the American "Shingle style."

The Shingle style represents a detour from the main road of decorative-window development, partly because it featured small-paned, mullioned sash, and partly because it was mostly a style for those who could afford a dreamy cottage on a massive scale. However, in addition to being great American architecture, its development shows how quickly one "style" gave birth to another during the late nineteenth century. Even more significantly, the originality of this form is a clear indication that even while the Eclectic decades were building a head of steam, the seeds of wholly different, modern styles had already been sown.

Certainly, many Americans were aware of the Queen Anne style before the exhibition in Philadelphia, but most had not seen such a building firsthand. The British building, called St. George's House, received tremendous attention, and along with other exhibits—in particular the Japanese—provided the creative buoyancy to carry American homebuilding and American decorative arts through the rest of the century.

The American Queen Anne style is easily identified by the broad contrast of exotic exterior materials, and the spacious, hedonistic interiors. Brick or stone is used for the foundation and part or all of the lower stories, and is laid up as much for color and texture as for strength. Next, a wall of stucco, or clapboards, or fancy-cut shingles rises up and around steep gables, sprouting dormers, and in the later phases, massive, projecting towers.

Truly an Eclectic's dream, the American Queen Anne house of the late 1800s has from its inception brought tears to the eyes of architectural scholars. This free classic style is a precise reflection of its vicissitudinous times, however, and as such, is a serious and unpretentious step in the self-determination of American architecture.

An important aspect of the Queen Anne style was that it provided architects and builders with the opportunity to make highly decorative windows an accepted and ex-

pected part of this primarily residential mode. The often massive, always irregular shapes, piled together with skillful abandon, created a fenestration which was ideal for the inclusion of patterned, colored glass. Upper sashes, stairway landings, window and door transom lights, and especially all the oddly shaped and situated openings which sprouted around the intersections of roofs and walls were, more and more, filled with colorful, leaded mosaics.

The variety of decorative windows, like the individuality of American houses, was endless, but certain basic styles became dominant.

The basic dichotomy separated designs into either

68. Plate 131 from Franz Sales Meyer's *Handbook of Ornament*, 1892. Elements from these Renaissance designs are found in many American windows.

"patterns" or "pictures," and in both categories, the color, complexity, and composition varied tremendously. As with any art form, the "best" examples were not necessarily those which are the biggest, brightest, or brashest, and pictures and patterns were integrated as often as they were formed as separate compositions. In both styles, however, the hallmark of quality American glasswork was the agility of the mosaic design; the determined effort of the glass artist to replace painted lines with lead cames, variegated color, and textural interest.

Picture windows, with flowers, foliage, birds, and animals, all created from mellow, colored light, are America's great contribution to stained-glass art. Pattern windows often reflect the popular decorative motifs found on furniture, household furnishing, and even industrial equipment. Thus, while decorative glass can often be related to the buildings in which it is found, the precise antecedents of many windows are just as often found outside architecture.

American pattern windows of the 1880s and 1890s can be subdivided into designs which emphasize either geometric or curvilinear shapes. The geometric style was primarily inspired by the English Aesthetic movement, and the curving forms were drawn out of nineteenth-century European "Renaissance" designs. Both these styles had been introduced before the centennial, but just as with Queen Anne architecture, their popularity didn't become widespread until after the international exposure in Philadelphia. Then for the next twenty years, variations on these two window styles became the most popular varieties of residential stained glass in the United States.

The American version of the Aesthetic movement was influenced strongly by Charles Lock Eastlake and Bruce J. Talbert, both of whose writings appeared here in the early 1870s. Eastlake's most popular book was *Hints on House-hold Taste*, which was published in London in 1868, arrived in America in 1872, and became an instant success. Trained as an architect, Eastlake is much better remembered for his writings than his buildings. In his own time, however, he came to see his best ideas so grossly manipulated by supposedly admiring Americans, that he finally exclaimed:

> ...I feel greatly flattered by the popularity which my books have attained in America, but I regret that their author's name should be associated there with a phase of taste in architecture and industrial arts with which I can have no real sympathy and which by all accounts seems to be extravagant and *bizarre*...[14]

This denial of guilt from association actually reads as an understatement when one compares Eastlake's emphasis on basic forms and "realistic" ornamentation to the products which emerged from American furniture manufacturers, and the suppliers of architectural decorations. In combination, this new mode was a delight for Americans but an embarrassment for a man who supported simplicity rather than complexity, and Eastlake felt little pride in knowing that a whole building style, encrusted with embellishments, was carrying his name. On top of it all, this style was sometimes promoted under the stunning malapropism "East Lake," thereby transmuting a sensitive personality into the anonymity of a back street in Anytown, USA.

Fortunately, the anonymity of residential stained glass has meant that to no window style has yet been attributed the misnomer "Eastlakeian" and it would be most inappropriate to begin now.

Crass commercialism aside, nineteenth-century Americans were sincerely concerned about quality building and quality furnishings, and overall, did foster an educated interest in all aspects of home improvements. They studied and applied the ideas of other tastemakers, such as Bruce J. Talbert, a Scotsman whose talent for rendering domestic interiors in minuscule detail propelled him, via the miracle of modern printing and intercontinental distribution, into a position of worldwide recognition. Talbert's first book was *Gothic Forms Applied to Furniture, Metal Work, and Decoration for Domestic Purposes*, and was printed in the United States in 1873. His second work, *Examples of Ancient and Modern Furniture, Metal Work, Tapestries, Decorations, Etc.*, was also printed in Boston in 1877.[15] Together, these deftly illustrated volumes speak directly to the questions of quality, beauty, and honesty, as would be applied to the household of anyone who aspired to an elevated degree of culture.

Specifically, Talbert emphasized:

> ...simplicity of design, honest display of construction, economic use of materials, [and concern for] framing more horizontal and vertical...[16]

And although he spoke primarily about furniture construction, these tenets could be used to describe precisely the characteristics of Aesthetic windows, where geometry predominates, the mosaic is fairly large scale, and the design is a powerful, yet simple combination of straight lines and circles. Simultaneously, Talbert would rather see a "free style" than an "elaborate reproduction of the past," and one would like to think that if he were aware of some of the windows being created in America in the late 1800s, he would have approved very much of their direct, yet subtle power.

Talbert also goes to considerable length to rationalize the introduction of curvilinear forms into the domestic scene, for his basic belief that "...cutting of straight grained wood into wanton curves, is opposed to the common sense..." is eventually mellowed by an acceptance that at least "...the ever changing curves of those for whose use the rooms are intended, will supply a sufficiency

69. American Aesthetic windows feature geometric patterns and complex multiple borders. This example dates
from the 1880s and uses cathedral, flashed, and opalescent
glass liberally sprinkled with jewels.

70. A stunning two part sidelight, c. 1885. The
flowers and torch are drawn from Roman and
Renaissance motifs, while a stylized Greek palmette and Egyptian sun disk make up the base of
the composition.

71, 72. More illustrations from Meyer, which can be found translated into American decorative glass.

of graceful line...."[17] Out of this, one begins to see the difference between the sometimes staid English Aesthetic and its principal contemporary, the curvaceous and flamboyant Renaissance style. In Europe, these two concepts were literally civilizations apart, but in America, they came to exist very happily side by side. It is, however, one of the great ironies of the Gilded Age that what Americans frequently refer to as "Victorian," actually is an interpretation of a lot more than just English taste.

The American decorative style known as "Renaissance" was inspired by the creative forms of several countries—in particular, France, Germany, and Italy. It contrasts strongly with the Aesthetic style, and for every straight line, sharp angle, and geometric shape of the English forms, the Renaissance style has a curve, a volute, or an arabesque. Other distinctly Greek and Roman forms are found, in particular the shell, or fan shape, and classical urns, out of which spring stylized floral motifs. The curvilinear movement of these Renaissance designs also creates, almost naturally, heart shapes, as well as the fleur-de-lis.

The royal French lily derived from late Gothic design, but it has strong ancient antecedents, and its multipart form offered tremendous opportunities for creative variations in nineteenth-century residential stained glass. Indeed, the fleur-de-lis would continue into the twentieth century as one of the most frequently found design elements in American decorative windows.

Like Aesthetic pattern windows, Renaissance pattern stained glass emerged in the late 1870s in response to the increasingly obvious potential for complex, mosaic glasswork. America's great cultural mix was not concerned that the fifteenth-century Italian Renaissance had arrived late to Great Britain and had always been considered a guest among Gothic peers. More importantly, late nineteenth-century America saw its own decorative history as an extension of "Wrenaissance" design, Georgian Classicism, and more recently, the strong, indigenous effort to reflect ancient Greece. Thus, the adaptation of classic Renaissance elements into contemporary stained glass occurred quickly, once the general decorative style had made its appearance in architecture and high-quality home furnishings.

In the best examples of American Renaissance stained glass, the entire window is a tightly woven arabesque, featuring swirling leads which end in paisleylike patterns, and which are frequently accentuated by jewels. Where multipart forms such as the shell or fleur-de-lis are featured, their individual pieces of glass produce powerful images in which the shape is fractured, yet the complete form is powerfully evident within the frozen plane of liquid light.

Probably the best place to find examples of the Renaissance style, as interpreted by American stained-glass artists, is in the *Handbook of Ornament*, published by Franz Sales Meyer in Germany in 1888, and reprinted by Dover Publications in 1957. Here are numerous examples of "Renascence" designs from many European countries, and while none are shown as applying specifically to designs for decorative windows, this book makes the creative backgrounds of American immigrant artists become very clear. The time frame of this publication also indicates that the popularity of these highly decorative designs was established some years before the first editions; likewise, the style was undoubtedly waning when the last edition was published in 1892.

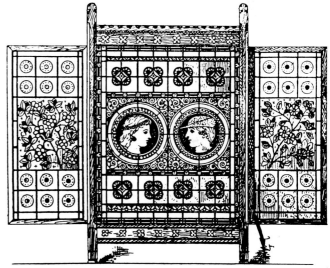

A decade before Meyer's book, an interesting English stained-glass catalog appeared, issued by the firm of Cox & Sons, London.[18] This 1876 publication provides an extensive selection of the sort of windows which were popular in England at that time, and it is easy to see how they differ from the predominant styles of the Continent, or North America. Designs which are specifically Medieval are offered for both homes and churches, and it is interesting to note the complexity of the leading, after watching the simple, large piece patterns of the 1860s. Painted glass is emphasized with many figural windows represented, and every design is at least partially hand-colored and fired.

The English have always utilized roundels, or the larger bull's-eyes, in their window designs, and the windows shown by Cox & Sons use these special inserts both singularly and in clusters. There are also examples of Queen Anne sash filled with a variety of glasswork, and as one would expect, a wonderful display of medallion-style panels. This catalog was certainly one of the better design books published before the late 1880s, and while the "American style" Aesthetic window was not shown, several of the specific design elements do eventually show up on this side of the Atlantic.

73, 74, 75, 76. The catalogue of Cox & Sons, 1876, showed typical nineteenth-century English stained glass. The Aesthetic style predominates. Note the owl panel (fig. 76) that later appears in Holly's *Modern Dwellings*, 1878 (see fig. 88).

Also in 1876, Charles Booth published *Memorial Stained Glass Windows,* which is probably the first American book specifically on stained glass. Booth was trained in England, and the cover of his small book is very much in the manner of something which would have been done by Cox & Sons. Unfortunately, it does not include any illustrations, although he specifically mentions "quarries," "geometrical patterns," "fillets," and "medallion windows." Unfortunately, too, most of his thoughts are on ecclesiastical work, although he does have some encouraging thoughts on domestic utilization:

> The varied resources of glass-staining are equally suitable for the decoration of mansions, affording a rich adornment for the windows of halls, corridors, stair-cases, libraries, dining-rooms, bath-rooms, etc., and in many cases effectually screening the objectionable sights at the back of the house. For these purposes simple and beautiful patterns of rich colors may be provided at very moderate expense. But where the expense will permit, it is surprising what beautiful effects can be had by the introduction of figures, birds, animals, and rich foliated decorations of all styles and grades, through which the light streams with a mellow softness which cannot be got otherwise.[19]

Later, in his concluding remarks, Booth also states that "…I have often felt that some…elementary knowledge of painted glass and its capabilities is all that is wanting to insure its adoption by the public on a far larger scale than at present…,"[20] and this comment is a good indication that even in the late 1870s, interest in fancy, domestic windows was still somewhat latent. This observation is reinforced by American pattern books of the same period, which are the best indicators of prevailing architectural taste, and which also show that the greatest era of American stained glass had not quite yet arrived.

"If any one firm in American architectural history might be cited as contributing most to the democratization of the late nineteenth century domestic ideas, that firm must surely be Palliser, Palliser and Company." So states Michael A. Tomlan in his introduction to George Palliser's *Model Homes for the People,* first published in 1876 and reprinted by the American Life Foundation in 1978. This was the first of many Palliser books and represented the start of a very successful system which emphasized illustrations, but which was also prepared to provide full architectural drawings to eventual clients. Palliser's first book was actually more a catalog of what the firm could offer, and did not recommend specific decorative details. Nevertheless, it is interesting to see the styles of the house which Palliser projected as "most popular," and one would expect most of them to contain some sort of decorative glass. This possibility is made more evident by the advertisement at the back of the book, for the W. F. Swords Company who offered "…Stained, Cut and Ornamental Glass of any description furnished at short notice…"[21]

In 1878, Palliser and Palliser published their *Model Homes,* which contained "…designs which have been made by us in the past few months, and with one or two exceptions are now in progress of erection."[22] Further, the authors stated that these designs show "…the ideas and requirements of a number of different individuals, localities…and show that progress has been made in the last few years in American architecture." It is also with this pattern book that a great change occurs in the windows of featured houses, for they are at last rendered to show decorative glazing, rather than just blank, unfathomable panes of glass. Almost every building featured here shows at least the use of the Queen Anne-style window, with multi-colored rectangles, and additionally, there is, for the first time, a detailed discussion of the use of residential stained glass.

77. The title-page illustration from *Memorial Stained Glass Windows* by Charles Booth, 1876. This was probably the first American book about stained glass. Unfortunately, there were no other illustrations, but the portrait window (fig. 14) shows Booth's style.

78, 79, 80. Typical American houses illustrated in Hussey's pattern book of 1876. The forms are familiar, but there are still no decorative windows. The ad for Tilghman's Sand Blast Works, which appeared at the back, indicates the popularity of ornamental glass, however.

Palliser begins by making an unabashed pitch for the philosophy of Eclectic building by commenting that:

Symmetry applied to private architecture is an invention that has had its day and is completely run out, except in rare cases, where old fogyism holds the sway and rules supreme.[23]

Then, in notes accompanying an illustration of a Stick-style residence, the author explains that:

The windows in the hall and staircase are filled entirely with ornamental and stained glass, as are also those in the attic; the other windows in the house have the lower sash glazed in two lights of ordinary glass, while the upper sash has a white light in centre and small colored light on each side...[24]

In concluding the description of this house, Palliser provides additional insight into American architectural perceptions of the period when he tells us this "cottage" was:

...painted venetian red, trimmed with Indian red, the chamfers, cut and sunk work being picked out in black, making it very effective and showing the detail boldly. The cost is $1,460, and we doubt if there is anyone who can show a prettier house, either in arrangement or appearance for the same price.

Blessed are they who have homes!

Let every man strive to own a home.[25]

Farther on, Palliser shows another "charming cottage" where stained glass is "…introduced in all the windows above the transom…," but he adds that this is "…a new feature for this part, and one which is to become very popular in all domestic buildings from this time forward…"[26]

81. An advertisement from George Palliser's *Model Homes For the People*, 1876.

In 1878, Henry Hudson Holly wrote *Modern Dwellings in Town and Country,* which the author hoped would "prove a practical and reliable guide for those persons who wish to build, furnish, and beautify their houses without an extravagant outlay of money."[27] More than just a compilation of plates showing various house designs, this book was organized into chapters which covered every phase of home construction from the "Economy of Country Life" and "Legitimate Woodwork," to "The Billiard Room" and "Plumbers Blunders."

Hints aplenty for all the would-be homeowners eager to be a part of the great building booms rising up across the country, and practical, down-to-earth advice at that. Holly's book is rich with effervescent promotion of his own work, counterbalanced by frightening tales of woe that befell those who would not heed professional architects who "…should stand to his client in very much the same relation as the physician to his patient…"[28]

In the matter of an "American" architectural style, Holly also had some interesting comments:

…we cannot be said to have any styles and systems peculiarly our own. In the absence of such, we have been too apt to use, inappropriately, the orders of foreign nations…Yet out of our necessities there have grown certain idiosyncrasies of building which point toward an *American style.* Doubtless we may introduce from abroad methods of design which meet our requirements, but we must not hesitate to eliminate those portions for which we have no use, or to make such additions as our circumstances demand…

…[These styles] are described…somewhat as follows: "The Queen Anne revival shows the influence of the group of styles known as the Elizabethan, Jacobite, and the style of Francis I, which are now indeed to be arranged under the general head of 'free classic'; but it has also been influenced by what is known as the 'cottage architecture' of that period."…

…In this way we are doubtless building up an architecture of our own, profiting as other founders of style have done, by precedents in older countries…[29]

Specifically on residential stained glass, Holly also had a good bit to say:

In windows only intended to give light, and not in a position to command a view, it would be proper to use small panes, or even stained glass with leaded sash. This would be allowable, for instance, in windows over a staircase landing, and indeed, in all sashes above the height of the eye.

Staircase windows particularly offer an opportunity for stained glass. When they are placed above a landing, thereby coming into a central position between the two stories, they serve a double purpose of lighting both, as is shown in several of these designs. When introduced in a

82. Palliser, 1878, Plate X: "...the stained glass work introduced in all the windows above the transom is a new feature for this part, and one which is to become very popular in all domestic buildings from this time forward..."

The year 1880 saw the *Specimen Book of One Hundred Architectural Designs* published by Bicknell and Comstock. This was really a compendium of designs drawn from other pattern books, and although no decorative windows are shown, there is a full-page ad in the back for the "New York Sand Blast Works," which specialized in ornamental glass.[32]

In 1881 William Comstock brought out *Modern Architectural Designs and Details* because, the author stated, "So radical a change [in Architecture] made it seem necessary to give a large number of complete designs for houses, as well as details of detached portions..."[33] This

proper hall...stained glass is appropriate, even if not admitted to any other part of the house. In the panels of the hall door, also, instead of having the unmeaning and at the same time expensive material, known as figured glass... stained glass would be appropriate, as its obscured effect would serve the purpose of preventing passersby from seeing in...upon the fan lights it would also be well applied...

Stained glass in our houses seems such an innovation that the majority of the people, taking custom only as their guide, are astonished at the mere suggestion; and, true to the religious instinct of their forefathers, who so long banished it from their temples of worship, it seems difficult for them to become reconciled to it in their dwellings.

The chief objection urged against stained glass is its expense; and although but a portion of the sash needs be thus treated, a dollar and upward per foot (according to the work) soon amounts to a sum which an economical estimate will not permit. Variations, however, may be given to an upper sash of clear glass, by making the sides of geometric patterns; and with a simple transparency suspended in its center, a good effect is often produced.[30]

The actual windows shown in Holly's illustrations are mostly of the medallion variety, but a number depict the beginning of much more decorative designs. The windows in one library show some very fine small work, and illustration of the dining room in another house has some realistic floral designs. Most interesting are the stained-glass sidelights of this room, for they depict *Day and Night*, and are lifted directly from Cox & Sons' catalog.[31]

83. Advertisement in Bicknell and Comstock's *Specimen Book of 1880.*

84. Compare this window, c. 1875, with figure 89, which is an illustration from *Modern Architectural Designs and Details* by William Comstock, 1881. The use of stenciled paint and geometric patterns indicates that the age of dazzling windows had not yet quite arrived.

85. A strong, mellow, Neo-Classical window, c. 1895, perhaps by Louis Comfort Tiffany. Unusual pastel glass, exemplary leading, and an effective use of jewels.

"radical change," he explains, had occurred because "The French,...has been supplanted by our present modified Gothic, which appears as 'Queen Anne', 'Elizabethan', 'Jacobean', or 'Colonial', and is a revival of the old Gothic...the present styles, while bearing many characteristics of their prototypes, do not adhere strictly to any of them..."

This was ample comment on the dramatic changes occurring throughout American architecture, and an indication of the concomitant cultural shift was the fact that the preface to Bicknell's book was also printed in German. This book is particularly important because it shows examples of decorative windows which can be matched to extant examples. Most of these are simple geometric patterns, illustrated as suggestive of leaded glass rather than as ideas for specific designs, but there are also a number of relatively detailed mosaic patterns which are the distinct antecedents of many windows found in America today. In terms of residential stained glass, it appears that Bicknell was right on the cusp of "radical change," because the fifteen to twenty years following his book represent the high point of American secular glass art.

In 1887, Palliser, Palliser and Company published *New Cottage Homes and Details,* which contained "Nearly Two Hundred and Fifty New and Original Designs in all Modern Popular Styles." In the "introductory" to this book, the authors state that:

We present on the following pages, American homes of today, not of any well defined style of Architecture, except what may be termed our National style, for it would be folly for us, who live in the 19th century, a nation noted for its inventive genius, to undertake to transplant to this new country any foreign style which was perfected centuries ago, and which though eminently fitted for the age in which it flourished, is not adopted to our wants and times...instead there is springing up a National style which is becoming more distinctive in character and unlike that of any other nation as the American climate, life, economy of time and labor, requiring greater facilities and conveniences, with snug and comfortable quarters for Winter and shady porches and verandas for Summer...

...That the American people are taking up with great vigor the question of home building for themselves goes without saying, and each one should be stamped with more or less individuality so as to fit into and harmonize with the lives to be spent under its roof...

Speaking of home, what tender association and infinite meanings cluster around that blessed word: Home—the temple of love, the nursery of virtue, the circle of loving hearts, the playground of children, the dwelling of manhood, the retreat of old age. It is the place on earth where health can best enjoy its pleasures, wealth revel in its

86, 87. Some very ornate glass appeared in Holly's *Modern Dwellings in Town and Country,* published in 1878.

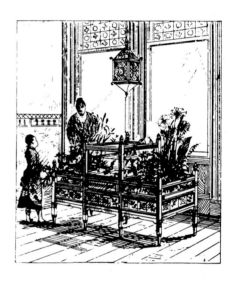

luxuries, poverty bares its sharp thorn, sorrow nurses grief, and dissolving natures expire.[34]

Certainly, the appeal of homebuilding was as strong, or stronger, than ever before, but by the time this volume was in circulation, the popularity of pattern books had already started to decline. There was competition from several architects' and builders' magazines, and middle-class homebuilding had also moved from an individual enterprise to a major commercial industry. Additionally, prospective homeowners no longer needed to rely on the assembled pages of illustrated catalogs to get ideas. They could see all they wished—in full-scale, people-dwelling reality—in every city and town across America.

If these factors had come together in a manner similar to

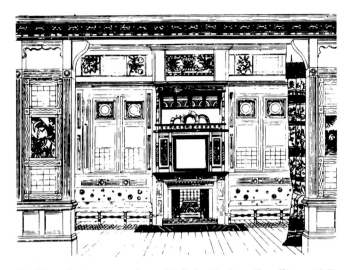

88. This dining room from Holly's *Modern Dwellings*, 1878, featured lots of decorative glass, including an owl panel (at the left) lifted directly from the Cox & Sons catalogue (see fig. 76).

turrets, *et ceterum*, as can be crowded upon the available expanse of wall and roof.[35]

Many of the houses in this book are of the Shingle style, and most of the others reflect a desire to move back toward America's Colonial past. Influence from the ever-popular Queen Anne is seen, especially in terms of window fill; the upper sashes of nearly every window are filled with small-paned, mullioned sash. In fact, the emphasis upon strongly rendered windows is striking, and there are a number of complex, mullioned designs and a few leaded-glass entryways featured also.

This strong display of windows is made even more interesting by a photograph which is included in the reprinted versions of this book (American Life Foundation, 1979). In the offices of the architects, whose partnership existed between 1888 and 1891, one can see several highly complex, stained-glass panels, one of which has a large, beveled oval in its center. Nowhere are such windows suggested in the buildings of Stevens & Cobb, and when

the events of fifty years earlier, when the nation was adapting the Greek Revival, then one could look at the pivotal point of the 1880s and carry the decorative forces forward to a specific and logical conclusion. The late nineteenth century, however, was far removed from the 1830s, and the fact is that while American secular stained glass was poised for its greatest period of Eclectic splendor, the main thrust of American building was heading in an entirely different direction.

This shows clearly in what was perhaps the last pattern book of the 1880s, produced by the Portland, Maine, architectural firm of Stevens & Cobb, and entitled *American Domestic Architecture*. The book was published in 1889 by William T. Comstock, and is a complete antithesis of the frothy, frilly building styles promoted by Holly, Palliser, et al. In fact, the comments of the authors on the subject of roofs is adequate testimony to the changes in architectural and decorative perception which were fast moving through America's built environment:

> Perhaps the one word which best expresses the correct principle to follow in grouping economically under one roof the rooms required for a given family is the word "unify". Don't playfully make as many jogs as possible in your wall-line; endeavor to reduce their number to the minimum. Don't study to contrive a sky line uneasy, full of antics; but contrive to cover your walls with as few planes of roof as possible. Not only does following this principle give economical results; but also the design studied with this underlying determination to unify will always be reposeful and grateful to the eye, in contradistinction from the restless effect of the structure designed with evident determination to evolve as many bays, porches, balconies, dormers,

89. Compare this window, illustrated in Comstock, 1881, with the painted medallion window in figure 84.

90. Palliser's *New Cottage Homes* of 1887 described this house as "...a fair sample of the American country house...recently built at Peekskill, New York, at a cost of about $9000. The first story...is built in hardwoods, principally cherry and oak... The transom lights to the first story windows are of art glass, as are also the top panels in front entrance and vestibule doors. The staircase windows are also of art glass..."

one thinks of the flamboyant panels—and houses—being simultaneously produced in Akron, Ohio, or South Philadelphia, it is apparent that soon such contrasting forces would clash.

Not all the changes in architecture occurred with such imbalance, of course, and some of the evolving residential styles were very inspirational to the creation of high quality decorative windows. These were the homes built for the well-to-do, and the *very* well-to-do, many of whom enjoyed ornate architectural glass. Queen Anne, of course, was a wonderfully flexible building mode, but for those who wished to live with a bit more grandeur, there were possibilities with the Châteauesque, Romanesque, and even Beaux Arts building styles.

All of these building varieties represent a sense of "high style," something which required the talents of trained architects and experienced builders. Often the best examples are public buildings, but many ideas incorporated there made an important impact upon lower level buildings.

Romanesque and Châteauesque buildings are of masonry construction, often laid up in great rugged stones. They can feature inlaid terra-cotta plaques, carved stones, or short polished columns, and there is an emphasis on the round arch. Windows are usually set in multiples, with separate lights above heavy stone transoms. Rooflines and silhouettes are dramatic, featuring steeply pitched, gabled dormers, and including round towers with pointed, conical roofs. Altogether, these imposing, solid structures are, from the exterior, extremely romantic, and generate

images of rich, sumptuous interiors which frequently feature ornate decorative glass.

By the 1890s the influence of the "Beaux Arts style," which can also be thought of as "Beaux Arts Classicism," was also making an impact on American architecture. Primarily a style of mammoth-scale public buildings, it was seldom used by residential architects, even for their most prominent clients. The exterior decoration on these buildings is sometimes overwhelming, but the impact of so many classical forms, in such colossal sizes and vast quantities, kept the elements of historical decoration and design in front of the public, in spite of themselves. The popularity and the impact of Beaux Arts buildings were also inspirational to the development of the Neo-Classical style of residential stained glass, and the huge display of this sometimes cluttered classicism also provided ammunition for those on the side of tradition in the Battle of the Styles.

By the 1890s, then, it was apparent that a new Neo-Classicism was intent upon retaking the ground previously lost to Eclecticism, but there were additional diversions which would shortly confuse the issues even more. These brand-new styles were Art Nouveau and the Arts and Crafts movement, and while each originated in Europe, they would, by the turn of the century, be making some impact on American architecture and considerable impact on decorative, residential glass. Although very different in origins, the American interpretation of these styles sometimes set them side by side; but whether together or separate, each style left a distinctive mark.

91. Palliser, 1887, design no. 103: "...the first floor is nicely arranged, and the large entrance hall will furnish up very good... the small sash and top half of the hall window being in Cathedral glass of many tints, would lend a very harmonious coloring to the whole; same in top lights of the windows of parlor and dining-room..."

92. An unusual window illustrated in Palliser, 1887. The mullioned pattern at the left would have been glazed with cathedral glass. The panels at the right would have been filled with finely wrought, decorative mosaic work.

Louis Comfort Tiffany and Art Nouveau

"Art Nouveau" was the name of an avant-garde gallery which was opened in Paris in 1895 by the art dealer Samuel Bing. Actually, this style of "new art" had already generated considerable interest throughout Europe, and it first appeared on the cover of a book printed in England in 1883. Art Nouveau is distinctive, with sinuous, flowing lines, highly stylized floral motifs, and often, sensuous female figures. It caught the fancy of an upbeat, European generation, and by 1900, there was a good deal of Art Nouveau architecture in several countries, with the primary interest emanating from France and Belgium. Eventually, America came to have quite an inventory of Art Nouveau stained glass, but little of the style was adopted for our buildings.

Art Nouveau in America should be discussed both with and without Louis Comfort Tiffany, the man who has become synonymous with American stained glass. The man and the style each represented new creative concepts, and each stirred up considerable commotion. In many ways these artistic forces are very dissimilar, however, and this is particularly true as regards the medium of stained glass.

Tiffany considered himself the originator of opalescent glass and the opalescent window style, and his designs are most often classically styled figures or extremely realistic natural scenes. Sometimes he incorporated popular Art Nouveau motifs, such as the peacock, and he was also closely associated with Samuel Bing, but one has to look very hard at Tiffany's windows to find any resemblance with what is otherwise considered the Art Nouveau style.

Conversely, if one looks at the whiplash curves and fantasized floral motifs of Art Nouveau, there is almost no resemblance at all to the great mosaic extravaganzas of Tiffany. Tiffany thought of his art as "new," and his glassware and many of his lamps strongly reflect the Art Nouveau style. But first and foremost he was a man of tremendous self-esteem, and it is doubtful that he would accept his late twentieth-century classification under a broader stylistic category. Tiffany is Tiffany, and must be given individual recognition for his great art and great innovations in glass.

If one then looks at Art Nouveau in America without Louis Comfort Tiffany, the scope and the impact of the style suddenly become very much reduced. This, however, is the realistic view, as little evidence of the style remains in America, with the exception again being extant examples of Art Nouveau stained glass. As a matter of fact, it is interesting to see so many American Art Nouveau windows, considering that they are so different from the architecture in which they are found.

One reason for the frequent occurrence of Art Nouveau designs is that the style arrived in America at a time when stained-glass studios were looking for more simplified, more easily constructed, and less expensive compositions. For this, Art Nouveau was ideal, as it featured large-scale forms with strong curves, and floral designs which could be broadly rendered. Thus, relatively simple patterns could be made to appear complex. Such work was encouraged by an architectural shift toward multiple housing projects, where a builder might order dozens of windows at a time, in a few repetitive patterns, and Art Nouveau glass could provide some pizzaz to buildings which might otherwise be quite plain.

Art Nouveau's main problem, however, was that it was just too avant-garde, too snappy and irreverent. The Establishment was looking for something to relieve the pressures of Eclecticism, but the style of the ultramodern was anathema, and the reactions it caused are still delightful to read: In 1909, for example, the *Ornamental Glass Bulletin* ran an article entitled "French Degeneracy," which said:

When Aubrey Beardsley had nothing else to do, he was wont to put a pencil to paper, and without withdrawing it, outline the figure of a woman. Sometimes he would thus draw the head of a satyr, prolonging the arms to represent limbs of a tree, foliage laden. He had a habit of twisting the torso in such wise that a portion of the rear elevation was to be seen advanced well to both right and left in the convolutions. This was his style in illustrations.

Over in Europe, France especially, a new school of architecture has much vogue just now. It may be called the

93. This window and transom are part of an Art Nouveau stairway-landing set. The vivid colors and carefully controlled shading of the background are typical of American glasswork in the early 1890s. The crude repairs indicate the unfortunate neglect that has befallen much of America's decorative-window heritage.

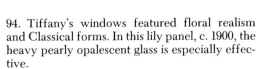

94. Tiffany's windows featured floral realism and Classical forms. In this lily panel, c. 1900, the heavy pearly opalescent glass is especially effective.

school which represents Beardsleyism in architecture. The exponents of this school, practically founded by Mr. Bing, have a way of fashioning adornments, exterior and interior, fashioning structures themselves in the twisted, impossible manner which Mr. Beardsley, following the windings of a vagrant pencil, placed before the world as Art productions.

"They call it l'Art Nouveau over there", remarked John Mead Howells, of Howells and Stokes, architects, in discussing this new method of construction and design. "It is really, to my mind, an evidence of a decadent style. It is a radical breaking away from conventionality, and has for its result many strange manifestations which lack wholly of artistic beauty, so far as my opinion bears weight.

"I am inclined to the belief that Burne-Jones and Rossetti and others of their pre-Raphaelite school originated this new Art. Beardsley to be sure, while but an illustrator, did many things which seem to be in a measure copied in structures I have seen in Paris. I would not say that they were actually copies, but they present the queer, twisted and distorted human figures, the oddities in curves and other outlandish shapes which violate all the canons of Art."[36]

"...canons of Art"—or more rolling thunder in the Battle of the Styles? Often, after comparing the reviews with the actual glass creations of the nineteenth century, it is hard to say. In the end, however, Art Nouveau in America was really just a flair across the clouds which were obscuring the upcoming, brand-new century, and it simply pales when compared with the masterful, realistic, figurative brilliance of Tiffany.

Louis Comfort Tiffany was born an artist. After he became interested in the medium of glass in the early 1880s, he embarked on an adventure in creativity which continues to be enjoyed by millions. It was Tiffany, along with John La Farge, who began earnestly to manipulate colored opaline glass, resulting in many new exotic varieties such as "confetti" and "fractured" glass. Tiffany and La Farge fell out soon after they had become acquainted, primarily because La Farge felt that Tiffany had taken advantage of their shared glassmaking knowledge. Little transpired between these two great artists after those early days, and Tiffany went on to become one of the great artist/entrepreneurs of his time, and probably history. John La Farge also produced fabulous glass art, but was never allowed to forget that he had given up an acclaimed career as a painter.

When Tiffany was at the height of his influence, his workshops employed hundreds of glass artists, who produced thousands of windows, lamps, and various *objets d'art*. He continued to supervise the operations, especially the manufacture of the glass, and approved the window designs, but his role as creator steadily diminished. In the early years, he did produce a remarkable assortment of glass art, and the surviving examples of his own work

express an imagination that was timeless. In many of his endeavors, however, he was neither the first, nor the most creative, although he was unquestionably the most persistent. Eventually his work came to overshadow almost all other American nineteenth-century glass art.

Tiffany certainly earned his reputation as the premier nineteenth-century American stained-glass artist who approached the medium with other than medieval instincts. However, though his style has carried forward as representative of an entire age, he only represents one aspect of American decorative window work. It should be remembered that within the period, he was but one of many strong, creative forces.

Arts and Crafts Stained Glass

As Tiffany and Art Nouveau were vying for recognition, another style was also generating much interest in America. This was the Arts and Crafts movement, which had originated with William Morris in England, and which would affect a sustaining influence in this country. Morris had organized a decorating company in 1861, and many of the artists who contributed their talents to the ensuing commissions, such as Edward Burne-Jones, earned significant personal recognition. Morris & Company, as it was known after 1875, became internationally famous, and was built upon a philosophy which was part medieval, part nineteenth-century socialist, and primarily concerned that handwork should be satisfying, well wrought, and beautiful.

English Arts and Crafts stained glass emphasized painted work, but by the time the movement had gathered momentum in this country, our preference for unpainted residential stained glass had become established. Thus, while the basic stylistic elements were adopted here, the design ideas were also modified by American artists, and the windows were frequently created from the multiple colors and textures of opalescent glass. More importantly, Arts and Crafts designs were often combined with elements from Art Nouveau, and even Renaissance-style windows. Eventually, American Arts and Crafts came to be identified with the early twentieth-century "Mission" style, which exerted considerable influence on furniture, home furnishings, and architecture. Some of the better known Americans in this movement were Gustav Stickley, Elbert Hubbard, and Will Bradley, and although none of these people was a stained-glass artist per se, they all enjoyed colored glass and featured glass art as an important part of their total decorative concepts.

American Arts and Crafts societies were well organized in the early part of this century, for the appeal of handiwork undoubtedly brought a necessary perspective to a culture which was fast becoming overwhelmed by the power of man and his machines. This interest in crafts and craft work has continued right into the present time, and is

95. This American Arts and Crafts window, c. 1905, features the familiar rose motif.

96. In the early twentieth century many windows were made in the Prairie style developed by Frank Lloyd Wright, the great American architect. This example uses crackle glass and some nice emerald jewels.

undoubtedly a key factor in the long-standing secular support of American residential stained-glass art.

Frank Lloyd Wright and the Chicago Exposition of 1893

Frank Lloyd Wright was one of America's greatest architects, and like other influential personalities, stands alone and above almost all the others in his medium. Wright is considered a Modern architect, but his nineteenth-century background impressed upon him the creative potential of decorative windows, and so many of his buildings utilize a variety of mosaic glass panels.

Ideas for the windows came from Wright, although fabrication was done by others. After a traveling exhibition of his architectural designs in 1907, many stained-glass artists picked up on his special stylization of plant forms. Thus there is a whole style of American residential stained glass which owes its inspiration to Wright, and examples are found throughout the country.

Wright understood the potential for decorative windows to be used as screens, or grilles, which could delineate space yet simultaneously be visually penetrated. His windows were set in zinc cames, which added strength and minimized the need for horizontal support bars that would be too easily seen behind the quantities of clear glass, and would take away from the verticality of his designs. Wright's use of decorative windows has been one of the few credits deigned to secular stained glass during the past fifty years, for his work is not considered representative of the nineteenth century. However, Wright's architectural beginnings are very much a part of the late 1800s, and considering the changes which occurred—and which he himself inspired—it could be said that America's new architectural century actually began sometime during the 1890s.

In 1888, Wright began working in the Chicago offices of Dankmar Adler and Louis Sullivan, two architects who had already developed a reputation for great imagination and individuality. Out of this office emerged some of America's most dramatic, bench-mark architecture, representing a new, Modern style. But the careers of both Sullivan and Wright were never smooth, and were sometimes traumatic, so these men led American building into the twentieth century quite erratically. Generally, they challenged established power, and more than once they were faced with the silence of an audience which had disappeared.

Of course, the country was itself changing dramatically, for by the mid-1880s the United States had become established as a national entity and a world power. There were still plenty of high risks and potentially big payoffs, but there was also by this time a distinct Establishment whose objectives were to consolidate and firmly hold onto their accumulated wealth. This Wall Street ideology brought significant changes to architecture, for as the successful people grew more self-assured, and conservative, they also became less ostentatious. And just as they brought their boardroom control to commerce and government, so they wished to see a built environment of symmetry, balance, and restraint. In 1893, this goal was dramatically achieved with the creation of the Chicago Columbian Exposition.

If people wondered why it took an extra year to prepare for the four hundredth anniversary celebration of the landing of Christopher Columbus, their questions were

97, 98. A typical residence and window detail from *Examples of American Domestic Architecture*, Stevens and Cobb, 1889. Well before the turn of the century, many architects were returning to Colonial and Classical forms.

answered when they gazed upon the incredible vista of the fair. Never before had there been such a display of mammoth, ordered, and synthesized building. Emerging from what once had been swampy lake shore, a fantasy of classical Roman structures rose up to create a sense of grandeur, solemnity, and order which was stunning by day and absolutely dazzling by night. For not only were all the buildings of Classic "Roman scale," painted immaculately white, but this was the first great exhibition to feature total outdoor lighting.

The impact of this event was immediate and long-lasting, and in many ways, architecturally stifling. People had seen a fantasy, created by the best planners and designers, and it was so real that it seemed incumbent to try and make it permanent. Thus, while men such as Sullivan and Wright considered the fair to be a great white hoax, the majority of architects, and most of the moneyed men, became once again immersed in the quest for the perfection of Classicism. Eventually this was achieved, for scientific techniques made it possible to duplicate exactly any ancient structure, but this ultimate success became ultimate failure, as it was soon apparent that the new century would be unforgiving to those whose thoughts dwelt continuously upon the past. The power of America's eighteenth-century heritage was made indelible, however, so although the ideas of Wright and other contemporary builders came to dominate twentieth-century construction, American classicism continues to share center stage in most parts of the country.

Decorative Windows at the Turn of the Century

The burst of Neo-Classicism in the 1890s was particularly evident in institutional architecture, and is best represented by buildings on the Mall in Washington, D.C. From the Lincoln Memorial to the National Gallery, the example was set in the nation's capital that the ancient orders, after all, could best symbolize the world's most progressive country. Many public buildings thus followed this Classic lead, while the main thrust of residential styles also moved backward, although mostly into the eighteenth century. Out of this "Early American" trend, there gradually emerged the ubiquitous "Colonial" home, which has since spread like architectural kudzu throughout the twentieth century.

Pattern books such as the one by Stevens & Cobb show that the appeal of America's early architecture had been recognized before the Chicago fair. Houses built in the style of the late 1700s expressed American nationalism and generated nostalgic thoughts, and could be lightly, yet elegantly decorated, which was an economic appeal to those who had saved the money to build. In the 1890s many homes followed a "Georgian Revival" theme or picked up on other Classical trends, but the style steadily boiled itself down so that, in the mid-1900s, any boxlike house with a hip roof and a meek pediment over the door could be called Colonial.

One reason for this change was the socioeconomic pressures which saw homebuilding become a major industry in which success and profits rested very much upon "building with the basics." Within this context, decorative windows were steadily phased out, not from public dislike, but because fancy glass was simply designed out of its most important forum: private housing. This happened gradually, but steadily, and unfortunately was accelerated by the stained-glass artisans themselves who continued to dilute their creativity until plain, leaded lights faded right back into small-paned, mullioned sash.

Between the beginning of the end, and the actual end, however, there emerged two important styles of American residential stained glass which tried very much to be like the architecture in which they hoped to find homes. The most prominent is the Neo-Classical window, which is composed of Greek, Roman, and Renaissance elements, superimposed upon a geometric background. Often these windows feature cathedral glass with opalescent accents, and variations of the Neo-Classical theme are endless. The most popular motifs found in these windows are the torch, the wreath, and the ribbon, and often, there are jeweled festoons, and at least one fleur-de-lis.

The inspiration for these windows came directly from the revival of Neo-Classical buildings, and as with other styles of decorative glass, they can be found in a variety of

99. Photograph of the Stevens and Cobb establishment, c. 1890. Note the very decorative glass panels. No such windows appear in the buildings designed by these architects.

100, 101. In the late 1880s, American residential architecture began a long transition out of the Eclectic Queen Anne, back toward a more orderly Neo-Classicism. This home, c. 1900, has a hipped roof, no tower, and no transom windows other than that above the front door. The fenestration is carefully balanced, except for the somewhat startling two-thirds of a Palladian window above the entrance. The square sidelight looks into a bedroom closet, but the Neo-Classical window fill complements the stained glass around the entryway. Note how the careful cutting of the glass grain adds significantly to the austere design.

THE FLANAGAN & BIEDENWEG CO., CHICAGO, U. S. A.

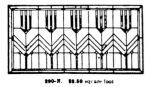

290-N. $2.50 square foot

291-N. $1.60 square foot

292-N. $1.60 sq. ft.

293-N. $1.65 sq. ft.

294-N. $2.50 square foot

295-N. $1.50 square foot

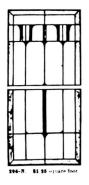

296-N. $1.25 square foot

297-N. $1.50 square foot

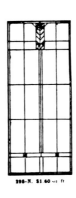

298-N. $1.60 sq. ft.

102. The 1909 catalogue of the National Ornamental Glass Manufacturers Association featured many Prairie-style windows inspired by Frank Lloyd Wright.

was comprised of dense, multicolored glass, obviously in deference to Tiffany. It was also created on a budget which related to a suburban house, so frequently the glass artist chose a broadly drawn scene, or some pattern inspired by Art Nouveau or the Arts and Crafts movement. Sometimes, too, the elements of the design were simply taken from the Classic forms, and leaded into uninspiring grids with mere diversions of detail and contrasting color. In fact, hundreds of these "terminal"-style windows are found in the pattern books of the early twentieth century,

PITTSBURG DOOR & SASH CO. 169

LEADED ART GLASS.

72. $2.75 per sq. ft.

73. $6.50 per sq. ft.   74. $2.00 sq. ft.

75. $4.00 per sq. ft.

76. $4.20 per sq. ft.

77. $2.70 per sq. ft.

78. $3.00 per sq. ft.

architectural settings. Also, the changeover was not abrupt, so there are many examples of interesting "transitional" styles which show how American stained-glass design began moving out of the complex patterns of the 1880s and into a more simplified mode. The key indicator here is the configuration of the background design, for in the earlier windows, each piece was usually shaped differently, while in Neo-Classical windows, the background is a distinct, geometric grid. Transitional designs also have more compact elements, and more gutsy glass. By the early twentieth century, great numbers of windows were using almost no colored glass at all.

The second important early twentieth-century style is best described as an "opalescent" window, meaning that it

103. This page from an early twentieth-century building-supply catalogue shows typical Neo-Classical window designs.

104. American Neo-Classical windows feature specific decorative elements set against a geometric background. The most popular motifs are the torch, wreath, ribbon, and festoons of flowers or jewels. Fleur-de-lis motifs also usually appear, which in this window, c. 1900, surmount strings of specially formed bell-flower jewels.

105. This interesting transitional window, c. 1895, has Renaissance elements set against a Neo-Classical grid as well as strong Aesthetic flavor in the border design. By the turn of the century, American window designers were struggling to keep up with the dramatic changes in architectural style.

106. Tiffany's massive opalescent-glass landscape windows were created for the wealthy, but in the early twentieth century middle-class Americans could afford modest scenic windows such as this example, which suited their modest houses.

HIGHEST CLASS ART GLASS FOR DOORS AND WINDOWS

RICH AND HANDSOME DESIGNS appropriate for dining room, front hall light, staircase light, interior and exterior door lights and windows.

THESE DESIGNS ARE HIGH CLASS in every sense of the word. They are made of carefully selected colored glass, as per illustrations, bringing out strong and harmonious effects. Such designs as these are sure to beautify your house when viewed from the street and add a tone of refinement and an added comfort and coziness to the interior, due to the beautiful effects produced by the light passing through these artistic color arrangements, such as are illustrated on this page. The various pieces of colored glass are firmly held in place by leaded metal bars made of non-corrosive metal and which will not rust or corrode when subjected to the weather.

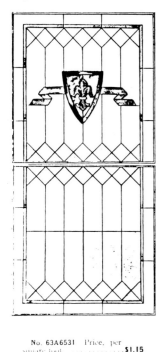      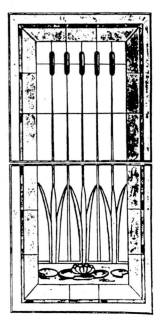

No. 63A6531   Price, per square foot $1.15

No. 63A6532   Price, per square foot $3.25

No. 63A6533   Price, per square foot........$1.35

LEADED ART GLASS IS MADE TO ORDER. Be sure to allow fifteen days, the time required to get a first class job.

107. When Sears, Roebuck and Co. began selling stained glass from their catalogue it was apparent that commerce had preempted art.

and it is unfortunate that the weakest and least interesting period of American glass has the most reference material preserved.

Well before World War I it was obvious that the interest in decorative glass was irrevocably fading, and there was no way to reverse the trend. However, there had been a few fabulous decades in which America's nineteenth-century glass artists had taken advantage of available materials and the great public support of individualistic expression. The glasswork of that time featured lush floral scenes, birds, flowers, and even exotic ladies, and along with showstopping bevels, and entryways and landing windows studded with handfuls of jewels, there had been an exhibition of creative cliff-hanging of the most self-assured kind. Unquestionably, the late 1800s represent the Great American Stained-Glass Revival, a period that was a wonder both for the creations that emerged and for the artistic barriers which were broken.

CHAPTER FOUR

Breaking the Barriers of Glass Art

The nineteenth-century American approach to stained glass grew out of a secular, decorative tradition, continued to benefit from a sense of free expression, and thrived in an absence of preconceived expectations. This resulted in important innovations in glass production, and dynamic experiments in window creativity. It also established American glasswork as an indisputably indigenous art. The new trails blazed by American glass artists sought maximum realism, and this goal was achieved by emphasizing the "real" qualities of the material itself. The resulting "American" style windows thus shifted the emphasis from paint and stain to glass and lead, and thereby formed the American legacy of stained-glass art.

The special qualities of American windows are the juxtaposition of glass color and texture; the imaginative use of a variety of cames; the inclusion of special decorative inserts; and the frequent adaptation of subtle or inventive fabrication techniques. Often, the best-quality windows can be identified from the unlit "street side," simply by recognizing the high-quality glass, intriguing textures, and a strong, sinuous web of leads. When backlit, a good window has the visual power to draw a viewer into the glass, where skillfully cut shapes, well-formed leadlines, and flashing jewels combine to capture and manipulate light in a multidimensional experience.

There have been various formulas for determining stained-glass "quality," usually based on the number of pieces of glass found in a particular panel. More pieces certainly represent more work, but that does not always translate into better work, so a more significant indicator is the shapes of the pieces and the manner in which each becomes integrated into the total design. For example, certain cuts, such as deep curves and sharp angles, are usually considered risky or impossible; nineteenth-century windows continually challenge such "rules" with very successful results.

Additionally, the American glass artists incorporated new combinations of color and texture without hesitation. They cut big, bold pieces with intricately complex perimeters, and minuscule chips which appear only as flashing sparks nearly buried within the flanges of converging cames. Altogether, in quality American window work, one sees each piece of the mosaic perfectly cut, shaped, and placed in a powerful, balanced design that bespeaks the total control of the medium.

Glass Grain and Shaded Windows

Beyond the variety of shapes found in quality windows, another significant hallmark of nineteenth-century stained glass is the careful and explicit positioning of the "grain"

---

108. Many creative precedents for modern architectural glass were set in nineteenth-century America, as exemplified by the so-called mercury mosaic windows that were developed in the late 1880s.

inherent in glass. The subtle, interior "flow" of color, texture, or just refraction, had been part of hand-fabricated glass since ancient times, but it wasn't until the late 1800s that this latent creative potential was emphasized. American artists set the standard for acknowledging and utilizing the swirls, the shading, and the shifting textures of their glass. This was particularly evident in floral compositions, where the luscious depth and realism of rich, streaky glass imparted a special dimensional quality to leaves, petals, skies, and clouds.

The application of selected glass grain was used not only to dramatize natural forms, but was also frequently employed to add a subsidiary dimension to geometrical designs. In opalescent windows, where there is a significant difference between the effects of reflected and refracted light, the background is often carefully cut from a single sheet of glass in order that the inherent flow of opaque colors is precisely preserved. Even more evident is the effect of glass grain in windows which utilize only clear, pressed pattern glass. Here, where many strong linear patterns are permanently embossed onto the glass, the correct positioning of these hundreds of individual lines becomes the significant factor in the ultimate success of the design.

A dramatic and skillful application of the color variations found in sheet glass is the American technique of carefully selecting background glass in order to create a distinct "shaded" effect. This technique was used frequently in the 1880s, but it later became too expensive to pay for the extra time and materials needed to select the precise piece of glass which would complete the gentle gradations of color built into the background of a design. When leaded up on the diagonal, color shading generally has the lighter tones in the upper left and the dark colors in the lower right. When the shading is vertical, both the top and bottom are usually dark, and the middle fades nearly to clear. Shading techniques represent a special factor of quality, and the number of such windows which turn up indicates the tremendous variety of colored glass available in the 1880s and early 1890s.

Special Leading Techniques

In the nineteenth century many studios produced their own cames using hand-cranked lead mills which took a thick strip of lead and extruded an H or a C or any other shape for which there was a die. A close look at the surface of old leads will often show distinct "tracks," or tiny, raised beads along the flanges. Occasionally, specially drawn leads were employed, with textures made to resemble the twigs and stalks of plants and trees.

It is not unusual to find windows which incorporate different sizes of lead cames, although windows set in mixed metals are unusual. The network of lead, zinc, or brass is nonetheless important to the total quality of design,

for good leadlines and good soldering provide the factor of "negative light" which is the catalyst for setting off the brilliant and sparkling motion of the colored glass. Good leading and good soldering also transform individual cames and solder joints into a sinuous, unified grid where the individuality of each piece of glass is magnified within the power of the total pattern.

Another technique used by American glass artists was to manipulate subtly both the lead and the solder to create effects which could not quite be obtained by cutting the glass. The best example of this is found with the "V" joints, or "pointed joints," which were employed to emphasize deep acute angles. "V" cuts in glass are difficult to accomplish, and inherently weak. More importantly, small, sharp angles tend to become obliterated by the width of even thin cames, especially when a layer of solder is also applied. The artisans of the nineteenth century, however, recognized that sharp angles can accentuate glass designs, and developed the technique of gently "pulling" the hot solder over the edge of the came so that it hardened into a tiny, sharp point.

Examples of these "V" joints are usually found where arching leads intersect, as in the center of a heart shape. In other instances, a window design will incorporate actual "right" angles, which appear to be cut out of the glass, but which are created by carefully filing out the middle, or heart of the came, and then extending the flanges over a rounded cut. When the two cames are soldered together, the design obtains a perfect 90 degrees, even though the glass is curved. Sometimes, designs called for a considerable open space between pieces, in which case the solder was pulled and spread over a wide area. Such "solid soldering" is often found around clusters of jewels, and also in floral designs where the width of a single came cannot convey the subtle variations in the thicknesses of the foliage.

One of the best examples of complex American leading is an unusual pair of stained-glass shutters where the basic pattern is a field of squares. Rather than have a series of right-angled joints, the glass was cut with rounded corners. which when leaded up, left small open spaces at each intersection. These spaces were then filled with fragments of came and the whole area soldered over. The result becomes visually intriguing because the leadlines intersect in a secondary pattern of tiny diamonds, rather than simple crosses.

Another interesting example of quality leadwork is the use of thin wires to create the illusion of cames. Some designs require extremely thin pieces of glass to complete a necessary but minute detail. Cutting such slivers of glass and then encasing them within even the thinnest came would not give the proper effect, and thus, wires were soldered over the top of a larger piece of glass. Examples of this work are seen in the peacock window. Notice also

109. This arched-top transom from the mid-1890s shows how careful cutting and leading could make glass grain a focal point of window design.

110. The subtle shading in this window from the 1890s required pieces to be cut from many different sheets of glass.

111. The "tracks" on the cames enclosing these jewels indicate that they were probably cranked out by hand around 1900.

112. Square cuts in glass are supposed to be impossible, but they are often found in American windows of the early twentieth century. They do set up weak points, however, as seen by the cracks in this railroad-car transom.

that the stamens of the large flowers on the left are also created with wires. Similar examples have been found in windows which feature stringed musical instruments.

It is not unusual to find leaded panels which have had the cames gilded. Usually the gilding occurs on only the side of the panel that faced the street. Gilded cames are found more often in England than in America, and such work is found most often on panels which were used around the front entryway.

Good glasswork usually has only two or three leads intersecting at a single point because the application of solder over several compacted cames results in bulky, unattractive joints. Where such groupings of leads were necessary, jewels or other special inserts were usually inserted, thereby eliminating unattractive joints and simultaneously adding a new element of decoration.

Subtle Support Systems

Lead is soft, but when it is soldered together in short strips around interlocking pieces of glass, it provides a very sturdy network. Many old windows have been virtually unattended since they were installed, and even though they may today be sagging, or have places where leads are missing, such leaded, mosaic panels are still surprisingly sturdy.

Most stained-glass panels were made with a secondary support system, however, to help mitigate the long-term effects of vertical weight and changes between interior and exterior air pressure. Traditionally, this support was provided by round iron bars set into the window sash, and the stained-glass panel was secured tightly against these by copper wires which were soldered onto the cames. This is probably the most commonly found support method, but many late nineteenth-century windows used support bars which were themselves soldered onto the cames. This provides considerably greater support, because the panel is being held all across its width, and it also eliminates the problem of the wires working themselves loose in later years.

Normally, support bars are set either horizontally or vertically, which can sometimes be distracting if the dark shadow line cuts across an intricate portion of the design. Often, in geometric patterns, the bars are set right behind jewels or other inserts. Glass artisans of the nineteenth century were aware of such distractions, and sometime modified the support system by running the bars diagonally, or even carefully shaping them to follow the cames around important sections of the design. There was even a lead came which had thin iron bars embedded in the heart, although this was not often used and then mostly for straight lines in the border areas.

Probably the least accredited support factor is the wooden frame around the panel itself. Frames are basically of two types, the sliding sash, designed to move up and down within the window opening, and the permanently set frame such as used to hold transom windows. The wood used in these frames was usually of very high quality: clear, straight grain, in thicknesses which are very expensive today. Besides being excellent quality, nineteenth-century window frames were often made from oak or walnut, and were frequently specially shaped and finished with finely joined moldings. It is also not uncommon to find window frames which were constructed from two different woods, sometimes both oak and walnut. This usually occurs on entryway windows which required one type of wood for the interior, and another for exterior decoration.

The window frame is especially important where the panel is an odd shape, and the American house designers certainly loved to invent unusual window openings. Diamonds, circles, arches, and even ovals are quite common. The amazing windows are those which practically defy description, and required significant woodworking skill to create. Not seen, and probably fictitious, is the window in the shape of a keyhole described by Sinclair Lewis in *Babbitt*. Whether such a window could actually be found extant is immaterial; somewhere, sometime, an American glass artist almost certainly considered the idea, and most likely more than once.

Frames should be thought of as an integral part of a stained-glass composition, and having the original frame in original condition is a key factor in understanding the window itself. Fine woodwork and fine glasswork are delightful complements, and the thousands of such examples emphasize the commitment to quality which is represented in our great nineteenth-century building heritage.

Large Figural and Scenic Windows

Large figural and scenic windows became quite popular in the 1890s, which was actually the beginning of the end of the great American stained-glass revival. Gradually both the positive and negative aspects of this style grew to overshadow the equally significant glasswork of the preceding decades. Usually made from opalescent glass, the big windows are best represented by the work of Tiffany and La Farge, although many studios across the country created competitive work.

The best large figural and landscape windows are designed with incredible detail and often include examples of exotic and unusual glass. When figures appear they are usually female, dressed classically and posed with classical architecture. Such windows were typical of the Neo-Classical buildings to which wealthy Americans were returning by the end of the nineteenth century.

The recent bull market in Tiffany's art glass has inspired several good books about these handsome windows. Not

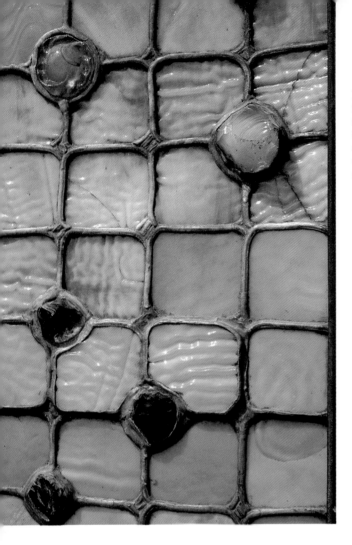

113. There is unusual leading in this panel from the 1880s. The cames were wrapped around each square of glass, and the diamond-shaped gaps were filled with lead chips and then soldered over. The rich opalescent glass and rugged chunk jewels add great textural interest.

114. The peacock's topnot was created by setting wires over the glass. The same technique was used for the stamens of the blue flower. Note the tiny air bubble in the bird's eye. It is an incredible detail in a figure that is only part of an entire window wall of highly ornamental glass, c. 1885.

115. The support bars on this floral stair-landing window, c. 1890, are bent around the beveled inserts so that they are hardly noticeable.

116. This heavy walnut frame exemplifies the quality of materials and craftsmanship that went into middle-class American homes of the 1880s and 1890s.

117. A double Lady Window, c. 1900, with Classical figures, foliage, and architectural framing. No Art Nouveau frills here.

118. The wheelwork of this exquisite cut-glass flower, c. 1880, was feathered out so that the background details do not totally cut through the red flashed layer.

all assessments have been positive, however, such as the 1972 statement that:

> ...neither of these men [Tiffany and La Farge] had even a glimmer of what a good medieval window should look like. As a result, their windows are without doubt the worst examples of stained glass ever to be executed.[1]

And even after five- and six-figure prices realized at major auction houses, many critics and historians are still not convinced that antique American decorative windows are to be regarded as significant art.

Floral and Small Scenic Windows

Flowers were the most popular subject to be rendered in glass in the nineteenth century, partially because their multipart forms are so adaptable to mosaic construction. Also, people of that era had a strong awareness and appreciation of nature, and enjoyed seeing that interest reflected in art and decoration. Thus floral motifs can be found in stained glass, beveled glass, wheel-cut and etched work—and every other glass technique as well.

Beveled windows, with their thicker glass and heavier cames, incorporate floral designs least often, with the shapes tending to be formed of shallow curves. Etched work, on the other hand, had virtually no limit on the degree of complexity or amount of detail, and there are examples of acided and sandblasted work which are as intricately composed as a drawing. Wheel-cut techniques were more flexible than beveled work, but more limited than etching, yet most panels included some surprisingly complex floral forms. Considering that each shape is composed only of lines and spots ground into the glass, the delicate touch developed by the glass engravers must be considered exemplary.

Aesthetic-style windows emphasize leaves as much as flowers, and the long, thin, sharply pointed foliage found in these windows is distinctive. Renaissance designs, on the other hand, incorporate circular flower forms and often have foliage blended into the overall background design. Artists working in both these styles often incorporated jewels into the floral pattern, most often as the point from which the petals would unfold, but in other cases, the entire blossom is comprised of a cluster of faceted glass. Neo-Classical windows used flowers often, but usually as a garland draped between other distinct, decorative fixtures. Sometimes these flowers will be strung individually, and include small jewels in the centers; more often they will be found interlaced with foliage and hung as swags.

Art Nouveau and Arts and Crafts windows also sought to interpret nature, and there is considerable contrast between these styles. Art Nouveau windows usually accentuate vertical designs and feature broad leaves and petals which can be tapered away into the hallmark "whiplash" curves. Such flowers are extremely lively, and appear to be growing vigorously within the medium of glass. Arts and Crafts flowers usually appear within an overall pattern, often set symmetrically around a window without accompanying foliage. Sometimes a leaf pattern is created without accompanying flowers. The best-known Arts and Crafts flower is the rose, usually presented in a squared-off form. As both the Mission style and the Modern movement gained influence, floral forms and floral designs grew even more simplified and geometric.

In the period of High Style American windows there were about two decades when some fabulous floral windows were created. Initially, these drew upon the Classical concept of a vase or urn, out of which emerged an ascending motif which included blossoms, leaves, and vinelike forms. Frequently, jewels were used profusely, both as part of the flowers and as decorative accents within the vase and the background. Small windows might be designed with a simple vase and floral arrangement that could fit into a horizontal transom light.

High Style American floral windows sought total realism and created lifelike plants, often in a semicultivated setting. Favorite motifs were the morning glory and grape vines, as these could be delightfully entwined across trelliswork which created a practical and stable window background. The great floral windows of La Farge and Tiffany are of course well known, but there were also many anonymous artists who took advantage of the lifelike colors and textures of American glass and created fabulous all-glass scenery.

Besides flowers, many American windows depict fruit, sometimes ripening on tree branches and sometimes displayed only as ornament. The natural scenes reflect the interest in floral realism during the High Style decades. Later, as part of the catalog of decorations used in Neo-Classical windows, the "bowl of fruit" became a popular motif. This was a colorful, arresting design which could fill the center of a window with ample mosaic action and still be easily connected to the grid of the simple, geometric background.

Fruit was normally depicted in flat glass, although the dimensional qualities of jewels was sometimes utilized for grapes. In stained-glass lampshades of the same period, other molded-fruit shapes were often employed, particularly for apples, peaches, and pears. It would be unusual, however, to find these special inserts incorporated in an antique window.

The American floral window of the 1880s re-created nature on a scale that caused viewers to feel as if they were standing inside a garden or sitting on the limb of a tree. In the early twentieth century, another window style appeared which made it seem that the telescope had been reversed: the emphasis on nature continued, but stained-glass compositions stepped back to the broad, "scenic"

119. This roundhead floral window, c. 1890, features wonderful streaky glass and jewels in all the right places.

120. Small scenic windows such as this windmill, c. 1900, were just right for suburban bungalows and city row-houses.

121. A grapevine transom, c. 1900, with opalescent glass and molded purple jewels.

view, where stylized shapes and forms replaced the details of individual petals and leaves. Tiffany's big commissions had made scenic windows the most publicized variety of stained glass, so it is not surprising that artists at the lower levels began to emulate what was then the most popular style. Thus, small-sized scenic windows emerged, invariably created from rich, multicolored, opalescent glass. Reduced and condensed, these compositions were quite appealing and fit snugly into the "Bungalow"-style houses which were emerging as an alternative to the simplified, Colonial cottages.

Stained-Glass Animals

There was a good dollop of whimsy in the nineteenth-century creative mind, and when it came to designing floral and scenic decorative glass, it was easy to extend the quest for realism into the realm of animal forms. Thus, among the leaves and flowers of many door and window panels, one can find a variety of creatures big and small, some created out of the mosaic pattern of the glass, some cut or etched, and others set as specially painted inserts.

Birds are perhaps the most popular animal depicted, which is interesting, given the difficulty of effectively rendering sharp beaks, long, thin legs, and the odd angles and pointed forms of wings. Additionally, a well-scaled bird often required some delineation of individual feathers, which was sometimes accomplished with paint, but just as often achieved by careful and exquisite cutting and leading of tiny pieces of glass. The peacock, for example, which was a favorite figure in grandly scaled, multipart, scenic stairway-landing windows, and was often created plume by plume.

There is great fun in finding other creatures of the forest, and it's possible to collect a whole arkful of different species. Check inside blossoms, between leaves, and watch out for spiders, bees, and butterflies. Other windows feature owls, ducks, and sparrows, and there is at least one bat panel in captivity, with the matching door still at large.

Many medallion windows feature animals, with birds again being the most popular subject. When ordering such windows, homeowners could have whatever subjects they wished, so it's not unusual to find dogs, cats, and other domestic pets. Then, too, the popularity of nineteenth-century fraternal organizations created another sector of decorative window demand, so elk, moose, and other symbolic animals were also created in colored, mosaic glass.

Stained and Beveled Combinations

In America during the 1890s, the Neo-Classical spirit began shouldering its way to the architectural and decorative forefront. Art Nouveau was considered pretty much an artistic upstart, and Arts and Crafts was keeping a relatively low profile. These styles continued to evolve separately, but each was a challenge to Eclecticism, and together they effectively squeezed out the freewheeling American glass of the 1870s and 1880s. During this time, however, there emerged the dazzling combinations of stained and beveled glass which represent the final, spectacular crescendo of American decorative window innovation.

Beveled glass had been historically expensive, although beveled mirrors had been available for over a century. The sudden availability of inexpensive plate glass in the 1880s, however, instigated an important trade in highly ornate, mosaic panels, made entirely from small, individually beveled pieces. These windows were often as complex as the highest style stained glass, and many were embellished with additional decorative techniques. Some bevelers incised tiny notches along the break line of the beveled edge; other times certain pieces would be incised with wheel-cut starbursts. Frequently, too, faceted jewels were liberally sprinkled about.

Several varieties of specially worked beveled glass have been identified including "honeycomb," "marvered," and "point bevels." Honeycomb and marvered glass have crystalline or circular patterns ground and shaped onto the flat surface of each piece of the mosaic. Point bevels were made by extending the width of beveled edges until they all fused together into a single point. Such beveled work is rare, but it indicates the degree of experimentation attempted in American glass shops.

Out of this tremendous interest in beveled glass, it was natural that pieces of colored and textured flat glass would be included in some designs, and by the mid-1890s, there had emerged stained and beveled combination windows which in the best examples are dazzling. This style of window is found throughout the country, but the best and most prolific examples are to be seen in the Midwest and on the West Coast. The East Coast cities were traditionally the originators of stylistic change, so while the Neo-Classical, Opalescent Scenic, and Art Nouveau styles were vying for position in New York, Boston, and Philadelphia, the cities and towns of the Midwest, and potboiling places like San Francisco, had a few extra years in which to stretch the Eclectic style to its ultimate heights.

Stained and beveled combinations range from the inclusion of beveled borders or beveled backgrounds to complete pictorial compositions where vases, columns, starbursts, and even floral forms are each created from many pieces of individually beveled glass. Sadly, by the end of the century, the whole spectrum of decorative windows was heading toward oblivion, so the phenomenon of stained and beveled combinations burst forth—and faded—in such a short span of time that they were hardly known long enough to be forgotten.

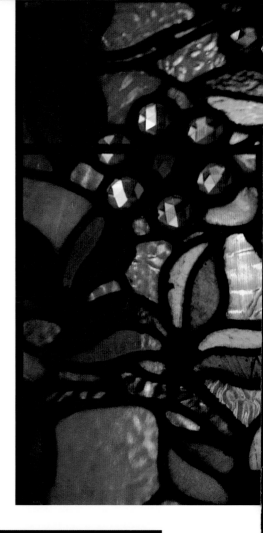

122. A late 1890s Art Nouveau rendition of the "Night and Day" themes that appeared in Cox & Sons catalogues and also in Holly's *Country Seats*.

123. Down among the flowers you can find a spider in his web in this detail from the splendid doors illustrated on the cover of this book.

124. An opalescent butterfly, c. 1900.

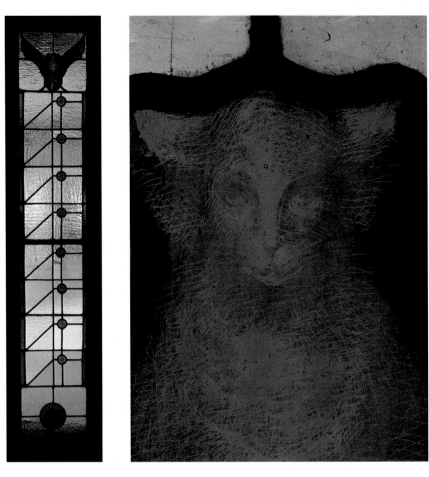

125, 125a. The other half of these bat doors is still at large. The design is quite contemporary. The cathedral glass and the shading techniques date this panel to the late 1880s.

126. Owls were favorite motifs in American windows of the 1880s, but pressed-glass figural jewels like the one in the top-right corner of this piece are extremely unusual.

127. The Midwest is known for stained and beveled windows. This one was made about 1895 and has a lot of Classical motifs in the background.

128. The top half of a double-hung stained and beveled window, c. 1890. Note the careful setting of the glass grain in the yellow border.

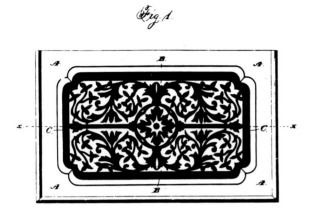

(No Model.)

C. D. PEASE.
ORNAMENTAL GLASS PANEL.

2 Sheets—Sheet 1.

No. 334,677.

Patented Jan. 19, 1886.

Fig. 1.

Fig. 2.

Witnesses
Jas. E. Hutchinson
Henry C. Hazard

Inventor
Chauncey D. Pease
by Pringle and Russell
his attorneys

129. This 1886 patent appears to be for a *scherenschnitte*-type window.

American Experiments and Innovations

In the late 1870s, near Hudson, New York, the noted American painter Frederic Edwin Church built a dramatic, Moorish-inspired estate he named Olana. Some of the windows were decorated with *scherenschnitte*, delicately cut paper which was sandwiched between two panes of glass. At about the same time, near the mouth of the Hudson, in Newark, New Jersey, someone else had the same idea. Instead of paper, however, thin sheets of brass were painstakingly snipped and hammered and used for decorative window fill throughout the house.

The panels found in the Newark house, like the paper silhouettes at Olana, have a strong Middle Eastern flavor. In one pattern, several animal figures appear. Most of the brass scherenschnitte was set into the tops of interior doors. Other brass sheets were glazed into Queen Anne sash.

Significantly, an 1886 patent has turned up which appears to reference scherenschnitte as a decorative window style. And other variations of American "silhouette" windows exist. In the early twentieth century, some glass artists cut figures from sheet lead and soldered them into the overall mosaic design. Windows with such silhouettes are a rare find, but they have turned up in both secular and ecclesiastical buildings.

Cast lead has been used on American decorative windows since the eighteenth century, either as rosettes, which cover the intersection of several cames, or as swags and other special shapes, which were usually draped or set between the leads. This application of lead ornament was used sparingly in the middle decades of the nineteenth century, but with the rise of Neo-Classicism in the late 1800s, "traditional" leaded windows again found favor. Thus, leaded "Federal" or "Georgian" windows needed to be studied carefully to determine their actual origin and age.

Examples of embossed or cast glass tiles can be found which range from 4 inches square to as large as 8 inches by 12 inches. These tiles are primarily floral, although some include birds. They are frequently found glazed into Queen Anne–style doors. Similar tiles have been found in Europe and even North Africa, so it is possible that in the nineteenth century, they were an imported product.

A more unusual example of figural glass is a large sheet of old amber cathedral upon which a number of forms are embossed. On this single sheet are ducks and a powerful, galloping horse, with each figure repeated so that a glass artisan could cut them out with ample background area. Examples of this embossed glass have yet to show up in actual windows.

A more frequently found American glass technique is known as "plating," and involves the leading of multiple layers of glass onto a single window. This process was often used in construction of major opalescent commissions, and windows have been found with as many as four or five layers of glass piggybacked upon one another. Usually, plating is found in two layers, with the second level of leadlines soldered atop the original contours of the design. Sometimes a single large opaque sheet will cover several pieces of the mosaic, as an aid in diffusing the incoming light. Sometimes multiple colors will be set in series, in order to achieve a precise tonal effect.

Plating was sometimes used in smaller, residential windows. This is usually discovered by the twentieth-century homeowner during cleaning when the dirt that has seeped between the layers of glass cannot be removed. Another problem with plating is that over the years, the extra weight of lead and glass will pull away, thus setting up a

130, 131. Brass *scherenschnitte* has been found in only one location to date, but there are enough patterns to indicate it was used elsewhere. These panels were originally set in the tops of interior doors of a house built in the late 1880s.

132, 133. The use of lead silhouettes is infrequently found in America, and so far, only in twentieth-century windows. The figures in this four-part hunting scene show wonderful animation and there is very subtle use of textured and colored glass.

situation needing skillful restoration. Plated church windows can be easily identified from the street, and are found with surprising frequency once their characteristics are recognized.

There is another variety of American decorative window which can be identified from the street, and is found in many areas, but which has a very mysterious history. These are the so-called "mercury mosaic" windows, or, as antiques dealers call them, just "mosaic" windows. Unlike the traditional mosaic glass, which uses metal cames or copper foil to support the individual pieces, the "mercury" windows are composed of hundreds of tiny, usually triangular, "tesserae" held in a bed of solid metal without further support. The amount of metal between each piece of glass is totally irregular, so it appears that the construction process required the glass to be set within a molten alloy, which then solidified. Usually, twisted copper wires are found embedded around the perimeter of each panel, providing a thin but strong framing to be set into the rabbet of the window sash.

The mysterious aspect of these windows is that neither their origin nor their precise process has yet been determined. In the *Scientific American* of April 1886, there is an article about a new type of window developed by the Belcher Mosaic Glass Company of New York which says in part:

Improvement in Stained Glass Manufacture

…We now direct the…attention of architects…and others to an entirely new process for making stained glass windows…

We refer to the work of the Belcher Mosaic Glass Company of Newark, New Jersey, whose showrooms are situated at 123 Fifth Avenue, New York…

[in the new process] The coarse, heavy lines of metal which usually obscure light and break up the unity of the design are wholly absent. It is, as it were, a lovely mosaic, built up of pieces of glass of infinite minuteness…

…The process of the Belcher Mosaic Glass Company is very simple and labor saving and permits a great economy in the cost of production…

There are some interesting pictures along with this account, which appear to be the variety of window in question, but no details of manufacture are given. However, the story that has grown up with these mosaic windows is that the process involved an amalgam of mercury, and that it wasn't long before the workers became contaminated and production was shut down.

These mercury mosaic windows are found in both houses and churches, some as simple, small transom windows and some as large as 2 feet wide and 10 feet high. The designs are created just like the mosaics of ancient Rome, with wonderful shaded techniques, and flowers,

134. This advertisement from the *Scientific American, Architects and Builders Edition*, December 1886, undoubtedly refers to the so-called mercury mosaic windows.

birds, and special figures worked up in tiny, colorful fragments. Frequently jewels are also embedded into various parts of the designs, and interesting floral effects are produced by allowing varying widths of solid metal to become tree limbs, branches, and stems. In some mercury windows, larger pieces of glass are used, and in other instances, sections of mercury mosaic are leaded together with sections of regular stained glass and lead came.

Special Decorative Inserts

It seems that anything which was colorful and translucent, whether natural or man-made, was at one time combined with colored or clear glass in some sort of window. Objects include seashells, pebbles, slabs of agate, bottle bottoms, and other "found" objects. Then, from the glass manufacturers themselves came dozens of different

135. An interesting window in the Queen Anne style displaying exceptional glass tiles.

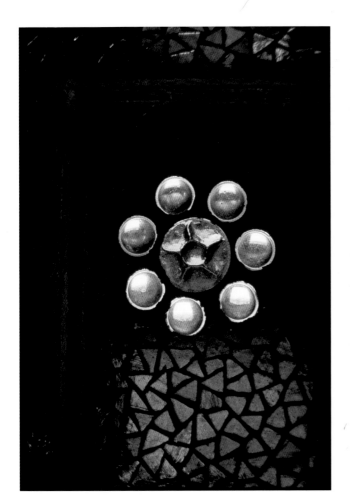

136, 137, 138. Mercury mosaic windows were made for only a few years, beginning in the late 1880s. They often contain unusual jewel clusters and usually feature glass shading. Complete entryway sets, as well as church windows ten feet in height, were done in this mysterious technique.

MVSIC : ROOM : WINDOW
BY : ALFRED : PIL

139. This illustration accompanied the article about Belcher's "Improvement in Stained Glass Manufacture" and features a mosaic inspired by ancient Rome.

forming the large discs from which sheets of crown glass were cut. The circular blob that remained had one side formed into a thick, sharp-edged cylinder and on the other side of this "pontil mark," the glass was formed into a smooth but pronounced bulge. When confronted face-to-face, this is very reminiscent of the eye of a bull—and several other "leave-them-alone"-type animals.

In the days when all glass was valuable, bull's-eyes were used to glaze small, unobtrusive openings, or were set in wide leads and used for "cheap" commercial window fill. Even during the nineteenth century, their quaintness was apparent, and old bull's-eye glass was much sought after. Today, heavy, thick bull's-eyes continue to be made in England, although their use is not prevalent in the United States. If real bull's-eyes are found in an antique window, their origin is probably European, and quite likely, English. They may also be newly made.

Roundels, on the other hand, are scaled-down versions of bull's-eyes. They were produced as a specific item rather than being a subsidiary of another operation. Roundels have just a little nub of a pontil mark, but often the glass has a very swirled grain. They are finished off with a thick ring on the outer circumference. Hand-spun roundels are produced today, but there is also a low-quality, machine-made variety which usually have a dull coloration, and the "pontil" mark is only a nubby little bump that was formed when the glass was pressed into shape. New, hand-spun roundels are often indistinguishable from old ones, and in the United States roundels are found in a wide range of colors as well as many special varieties.

The centrifugal force of the spinning process produces a natural "pinwheel" effect, and thus there are roundels which are multicolored, much like the old-time, all-day lollipops. Another variety has raised spokes which spiral out from the pontil mark.

More typical of American secular windows is the inclusion of what are usually called "jewels," which are made to imitate precious stones. They are found in a wide variety of colors, sizes, shapes, and special forms. The prolific use of jewels is one of the principal innovations of American glass artists even though the production of glass "jewels" originated in ancient times. It is not known when the first jewels were used in American windows, but by 1890 they were being incorporated into American decorative windows with completely joyful abandon.

The most desirable variety are known as "chunk" jewels, and have facets which were produced by chipping. This created primitive but elegant prisms. Chunk jewels are found as large as 2 inches across, and as small as tiny chips. Their occurrence in a window is not rare, but should be considered a premium. Whether large or small, they protrude from the surface of the window with great presence, adding dimension as well as textural interest.

"jewel" forms, as well as specially created inserts such as leaves, flower forms, bull's-eyes, roundels, and a selection of large, pressed glass tiles.

Today, the term "bull's-eye" has become synonymous with the term "roundel," although anyone reading contemporary accounts of stained glass may be startled to discover all the variations on how to spell the word. It has appeared as "rundel," "roundelle," and "rondel," which is most likely the reason why most people just prefer to say "bull's-eye."

Technically, the bull's-eye is the remainder of the hot gather of glass which was spun on the iron punty, thereby

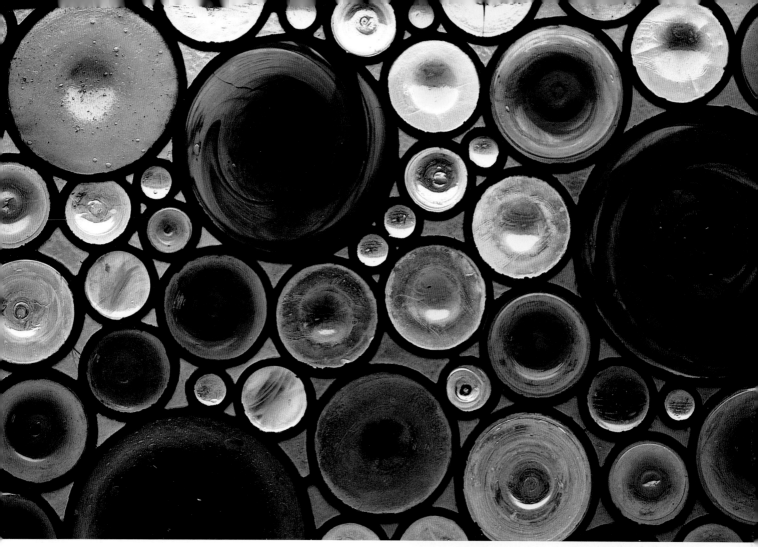

140. Roundels, rundels, roundeles—or bull's-eyes,
c. 1890.

141. Roundel windows, such as this 1890s
example, were very popular in Eclectic
American houses of the late nineteenth
century.

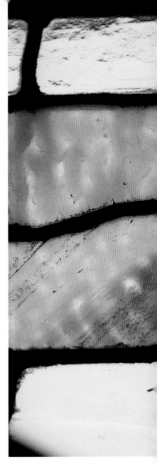

142. These unusual ruby jewels combine to form a dramatic three-dimensional star, c. 1885.

143. A colorful cluster of pressed and faceted glass combined with opalescent and cathedral glass.

144. A primitive and magnificent jewel from an 1870s church window. This is a detail from figure 148.

145. This diminutive door panel from the late 1880s preens like a peacock. Note the texture and grain of the glass and the three two-colored jewels.

146. Crackle-jewel triplets, c. 1885.

147, 147a. A stunning jeweled and beveled door panel that is as appealing today as it was in the late 1890s.

Other jewels which add greatly to stained-glass design are the "pressed" variety, found in a veritable catalog of different shapes and sizes. Also called "molded" jewels, they can be found as leaves, teardrops, pyramids, and multiform geometric shapes. There were also blocks of small square jewels pressed out like chocolate bars, so that a window designer could cut apart whatever multiples were required. Thus, one finds clusters of square jewels which are set with a single lead around the whole shape.

Some jewels were pressed by hand, others were created mechanically. In both cases, the methods were primitive enough that the old jewels have characteristics which are difficult to duplicate today. Just like old sheet glass, old jewels have irregularities and imperfections which create additional opportunity for light to be bounced about as it travels from one side to the other. In general, jewels are most powerfully used in groups or clusters, and many windows have specially designed combinations such as star shapes or circles which by themselves become impor-tant elements in the window's design. As with roundels, pressed jewels come in all tones, and are sometimes streaky, sometimes opalescent, and sometimes simply crisp and clear.

The best faceted jewels were cut and polished by hand, and have a sparkle and luster that sets them apart from the dull, machine-made variety. Such jewels add tremendous sparkle and flash to a mosaic composition, and there were window and door panels created in the 1890s which are basically all jewels, an overwhelming sight with their force of captured and refracted light.

In many designs, jewels are used as swags or festoons, often in varying or "progressive sizes" just like a string of pearls. Tiny jewels usually begin and end a strand, with larger jewels, perhaps of a different color, in the middle of the string. Jewels were also used to outline a particular section of a design such as special shapes leaded into the center of a panel. There is probably no such thing as a window with too many jewels.

CHAPTER FIVE

The American Stained-Glass Business

America's great attraction has always been the opportunity to achieve wealth, and in the closing decades of the nineteenth century, with natural and financial resources not yet preempted, and business flourishing under a laissez-faire attitude, economic activity became frantic, and sometimes voracious. The high rollers like Cornelius Vanderbilt and Jay Gould struggled to accumulate and maintain plutocratic power, and while the mainstream of American business continued to ebb and flow more democratically, the economic pressures on everyone grew more intense and less forgiving.

The effects of this widespread personal success were strongly reflected in the increased quantity and quality of residential architecture and were equally manifest in the development and expansion of commercial centers. The big cities, of course, set the pace, and the people there became accustomed to monstrous building projects before small towns saw local frame and masonry buildings rise more than a few stories. New ideas and new products spread quickly, however, and out of this hectic, nationwide activity, the wonderful architectural legacy of America's nineteenth-century downtown streetscapes emerged.

A century later these buildings continue to represent the basic commercial environment for much of middle America, and although the twentieth century has seen many of these Main Streets suffer from tasteless attempts at modernization, these business properties are now being appreciated for their fine workmanship, thoughtful planning, and decorative detail. When properly restored or preserved, the old commercial districts welcome pedestrians into a humanly scaled environment, where the clapboard siding projects a sense of stability, and honesty is reflected in the big display windows at street level. Often the old commercial and residential districts now blend into a single, multipurpose neighborhood, and many interesting decorative windows can be found here.

It is in these same areas that long-established churches are also located. Many of these were once important community centers and still retain exceptional decorative windows. In fact, old churches are often excellent "libraries" of antique glasswork, for one can sometimes find the total, basic chronology of American window art lined up in a large, well-lit space.

Just as with secular windows, however, the history of American church windows has been involved in a controversy that has been roiling since the proponents of opale-

148. These small church windows were made within a few years of the 1871 patent date on the vent mechanism. The rich glass and luscious jewels are exceptional. The emphasis is on nature and decoration, not religious symbolism.

149, 150 (*Above*: Boston, 1855; *below*: Philadelphia, 1879). By the third quarter of the nineteenth century, American architecture had made dramatic changes to window surrounds, window openings, and window fill. Commercial avenues had grown into public panoramas of new styles and decorative possibilities.

scent windows and traditional glass painters struggled to maintain economic parity at the turn of the century. This conflict is still not resolved, but at least the quality and significance of many American windows has been recognized. The next step is to have our grand inventory of glass art better understood.

Commercial Decorative Windows

Even during the middle 1800s the installation of large sheets of polished plate glass could result in considerable attention being given to a building and its proprietor. Thus,

it soon became apparent to both builders and merchants that the selective installation of mosaic or other decorative glass represented an excellent opportunity to advertise to a large audience in a very urbane manner.

The result is that much of America's nineteenth-century commercial architecture retains some interesting glass-work, the best examples of which are closely related to residential windows in both designs and architectural placement. For example, just as a residential transom light provides a "window over a window," many shop fronts have the transom area over the display windows filled with

151, 152. Whether viewed from the exterior or the interior, stained-glass advertising was a pleasing embellishment to nineteenth-century commercial streetscapes. This building was designed as a residence in the 1880s, and the Art Nouveau window with painted floral details was installed about ten years later.

153. This "Postmaster" sign was acid-etched from blue flashed glass in the 1890s. Also note the glue-chip glass in the background.

154. Windows of this type were popular in mid-nineteenth-century American churches. There is religious symbolism in the painted medallion at the top, but there is also a strong emphasis on nature in the stenciled quarries.

155. A transitional American church window of the early 1880s with neither paint, stain, nor religious symbols. Cathedral glass and some special jewels form a geometric composition that shows how secular designs came to dominate nineteenth-century glass art in the United States.

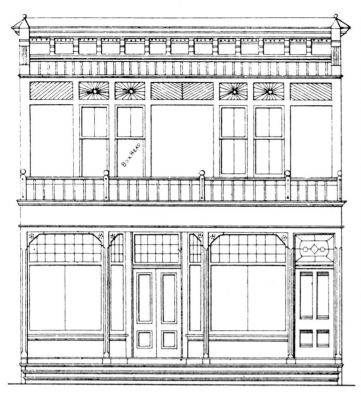

156. This suggested store front from Comstock, 1881, allocated space for display windows and decorative glass.

decorative glass. This heightens the effect of the fenestration, provides a bonus area for light penetration, and represents a custom-made framework for a commercial message.

At the street level, where there was maximum exposure and advertising impact, many commercial transoms were designed with the logo for a product or the name of the shop. Often, the lettering was done in opaque white glass and there was sometimes additional colored glass around the border. The prominent lines and letters of such advertising windows were meant to be quickly recognized and easily read, and the lettering was often set within a background of thick glass with a heavily reeded, or otherwise obscured surface. Due to the large areas of many of these commercial windows, such mosaics were frequently set in extra-heavy zinc cames, and further strengthened by thick iron frames.

Many transoms found in commercial districts are more delicate, especially where Main Street residences were gradually transformed into business property. Early decorative windows can also be found here, such as gilded transoms or designs "carved" out of flashed glass by either etching or wheel cutting. Often these techniques were also used for inside commercial applications, for example the famous O.N.T. spool cabinets with etched-glass drawer labels, or similar work found on fancy meat and produce scales.

More great glass can be found in institutional buildings. Old banks are particularly fun to visit as many feature bronze furnishings, antique lighting fixtures, and door panels with glue chip or other specially worked glass. City halls and old courthouses are likewise good places to find high-quality architectural detail. Even the monolithic institution that is today's Postal Service once used neat little etched-glass signs to identify the windows for stamps and parcel post.

The frequent use of decorative windows in commercial buildings testifies to the nineteenth-century belief that ornament added significantly to the overall quality of life. Consequently, a survey of the architectural details along most old Main Streets can be as rewarding as similar studies in historic residential neighbourhoods. Above street level decorative windows in commercial architecture are often found in multiple groups set in the top half of double-hung windows. Sometimes the windows along an entire top floor are glazed in this manner, thereby combining with the building's cornice to produce added embellishments to the roofline. More often, repetitive panels were set at the stairway landings, and it is not uncommon to find fancy oval or circular windows in such locations. Commercial decorating budgets were spent primarily for beautifying the "street side" of a building, but a wander down back alleys can also turn up additional good glass at the rear and at the sides of old stores and apartments.

It is, in fact, surprising how often fancy windows were made an integral part of commercial construction, considering that such building were financed as business ventures. But at the end of the nineteenth century, businessmen thought it proper that new construction should be adequately and sometimes elaborately decorated. People in general also believed that what was good for one sector of society also was good for another.

An example of this is seen in Palliser's *Model Homes* of 1878, where the "Design for a Masonic Lodge" could easily serve as inspiration for a variety of buildings.[1] The ground floor was designed as an income-producing retail store, and the upper stories could easily be modified to include apartments instead of the Lodge Room. Change the floor plans, rework the entrance and porch areas, and one could have a fine, stately home; or simply modify the towers and the roofline, and presto, there would emerge a charming church. Clearly, the elfin spirit of Eclecticism had a bit of inspiration for everyone, and in a time when the nation needed buildings for every purpose, it can be seen why this comfortable, flexible style caught the fancy of the nation. Indeed, in describing this building, Palliser makes it a point to say:

...The cost of this building complete is $3000; and we think

157, 158. Except for the dedication plaques, these Aesthetic and Renaissance-style church windows could have fit perfectly into an upscale residence of the late 1880s.

159. Palliser's suggestion for a Masonic Lodge, c. 1878.

that no country town having a lodge of Masons can afford to be without such a building as this, as by owning such a building, they are fulfilling one of the tenets of Masonry, besides being a monument to the taste, spirit, and liberality of its founders.[2]

Consider that phrase, "...taste, spirit, and liberality...." Such ideology sounds jaded today, but a hundred years ago, in the expanding cities and brand-new towns, such abstractions exerted a strong influence on the popular awareness that America was astride the cutting edge of history.

Additionally, Palliser's "Masonic Lodge" also presents an interesting link in the development of American decorative windows, for the description of the buildings also notes that:

...The east end of the lodge room is very neat and effective, the recess behind the W.M. having a circle head, with the round stained glass window placed in the upper part, in which is worked the all-seeing eye, and other appropriate emblems. The other windows have transom lights, filled with stained glass, in which is worked such designs as are emblematical of Masonry...[3]

Books such as those by Palliser and Comstock show that by the last quarter of the 1800s, secular buildings were the dominating reference for American architects. Thus, when a surge of church building arose, it was only to be expected that the influence of American secular stained glass would provide the impetus out of which our own styles of ecclesiastical windows would emerge.

American Windows for American Churches

In the 1840s, when colored glass was just beginning to find application in American architecture, this country had a strict heritage of nondecorated ecclesiastical buildings. This had evolved out of the conservative religions of the Pilgrim-century emigrants, and from the fact that between the seventeenth and the early nineteenth centuries, European stained glass suffered its most artless years. As a result, although the resurgent interest in colored, mosaic glass generated much interest among American church builders, the continuing European emphasis on figural symbolism, done in an old-fashioned, painted style, was simply not going to be instantly idolized by a culture whose thoughts were on the future, and whose God was sought more through nature than in ancient rites.

Even more important was the fact that nineteenth-century American architectural energy was directed toward secular projects, as often commercial as residential. In the decades before and after the Civil War, church building was literally left in the dust of a nation expanding in quantum leaps. The American church windows which survive from the middle 1800s are primarily comprised of quarried work, often highlighted with stenciled designs. There was some figural and painted work being done in this country, but most windows done in that style were imported from European studios. Significantly, these European window producers considered the American painted-window market to be their franchise, and that attitude would later instigate a traumatic clash with America's indigenous studios.

Between the 1870s and the 1890s American church windows evolved primarily as a reflection of the developments of secular, decorative styles. American glass artists had always been most inspired by the inherent characteristics of glass, and had concentrated their energy on the creative potential of multicolored densities, and the natural and artist-inspired surface irregularities. Sensuous variations of color and texture were juxtaposed and melded into new levels of glass expression, for the American style was to extract maximum expressiveness from the material itself. It was therefore natural that American artists would extend these decorative precepts into a new style of religious stained glass—a development they considered both logical and long past due.

Thus emerged the "American church window": strongly mosaic, composed of cathedral, textured, and select opalescent glass; liberally sprinkled with jewels; and featuring little paint or stain. Additionally, as secular styles changed, so did church windows, and one finds Renaissance, Aes-

160. An 1890s transitional church window showing how the neo-Gothic figural style began to overtake the decorative emphasis of the 1870s and 1880s.

161. Another popular religious style of the 1890s combined symbolic medallions with Renaissance decoration.

thetic, Neo-Classical, and floral motifs in the same forms as one would expect to see in the parishioners' homes. Indeed, Americans have always been wary of too many religious images, and the strongly secular church designs probably represent a successful compromise between those who wanted stained glass, and those who would have been happy to continue worshiping in pure, unfiltered light.

Beginning in the 1870s, these American-style windows were widely used in new church construction and ordered as replacements for the old quarrywork. This decorative style was not often suited to nor selected for cathedral-size buildings, but likewise, the European painted style was generally too overdone and too expensive for neighborhood and rural settings. Church building had increased dramatically by 1890, due to the waves of religious immigrants and a strong national revival, and there was plenty of business for studios working in every style.

While the traditional glass painters—both European and American—would have been delighted to see time stand still somewhere around A.D. 1400, the majority of American glass artists continued to experiment with new varieties of glass and new window styles. What emerged were the ecclesiastically nefarious opalescent scenic and figural windows, made entirely of American "art glass," with its internal fires and swirls of variegated color. When creatively selected, delicately cut, and imaginatively leaded into mosaics, these windows were as detailed and as artistically successful as if the glass had been painted in the traditional manner. But when the popularity of such windows began seriously to encroach on what the medievalists considered sacrosanct buildings—and their traditional economic territory—they called for a crusade against this infidel art and set out to defend the stained-glass salient of the Battle of the Styles. In the end, that struggle nearly annihilated everyone.

By the mid-1890s, it was obvious that Eclectic architecture was living out its last hurrah, and while ornate, secular windows continued to be popular, they too were heading for an uneasy ending. American decorative church windows were also evident in this stylistic sunset, finding a certain popularity in mass-produced, Neo-Classically inspired designs, but steadily giving up ground to both the traditional, painted styles and the new opalescent mode. Significantly, excellent painted windows were by this time being "Made in America," a development which further fragmented the opposing forces. Thus, for most studios, life in the economic trenches became a struggle simply to survive and defensively retain a dwindling market share.

Exacerbating the situation was Louis Comfort Tiffany, who actively promoted his opalescent glass as the quintessential American effort to give a modern dimension to a historically staid art form. But his business dealings were sharp, and he enjoyed too much describing his own work

as the best ever made. The result was that he made few friends in the glass community, and for some became a symbol of religious degeneracy.[4]

By the early 1900s the demand for Tiffany windows had grown to the point where a platoon of artisans was designing and installing them all over the world, although Tiffany himself was by then more interested in his "Favrile" glassware, and his copper-foiled, mosaic lamps. The strength of Tiffany's stained-glass position could not be breached in his lifetime, but when Tiffany Studios filed for bankruptcy in 1932, and Tiffany himself died in 1933, the forces of ecclesiastical Gothicism swept in and claimed victory over a decimated artistic outpost about which most people no longer cared.

The shade of Tiffany's artistic genius has remained, which has been good for the art market, but which has also caused the twentieth-century perspective of America's stained-glass heritage to remain focused on the debate between opalescent religious windows and the centuries-old tradition of painted glass. In this situation, it is important to put considerable space between the works of one man and a national creative phenomenon. For example, the inspiration for America's modern glass movement is a reflection of the totality of our nineteenth-century glass art, and just as the moon-rock window in Washington's National Cathedral is praised for its free-spirited expression, so should the whole scope of America's nineteenth-century antique windows be acclaimed for their originality and artistic bravery.

American Stained Glass in the Fading Years

The Stained Glass Association of America was organized in 1903, and the early history of this organization is the best-documented segment of America's stained-glass heritage. The memoirs of the old-timers and the candid, often vitriolic comments of the members provide an insight into how an ancient art was steadily transformed by American materials, styles, and techniques.

The roots of this organization go back to 1893, when The United Stained Glass Workers was formed, and petitioned the U.S. Congress for action against what they believed was unfair foreign competition. Their concern was valid, for English, German, and other European studios were actively seeking American church commissions and were receiving some tariff advantages. Trying to change import duties was really a tilt against economic windmills, however, for it was cutthroat domestic competition that was driving American stained glass toward bankruptcy. As the lucrative business associated with secular architecture dissolved, business became grim, and self-interest predominated. Labor costs rose, and stained glass could not look to mechanization to decrease manpower expense; prices might be raised, but then business would definitely be lost to studios who did work at cost, or less. The result

162. Large figural opalescent windows were very popular around the turn of the century. Paint was used only for faces and hands. This new style of religious window flustered traditional stained-glass artists because of aesthetic differences and because of intensified economic competition.

163, 164. A good example of an American church window is seen in the IHS monogram, c. 1890. The heavily jeweled dedication plaque also points up the nineteenth-century American approach to religious stained glass.

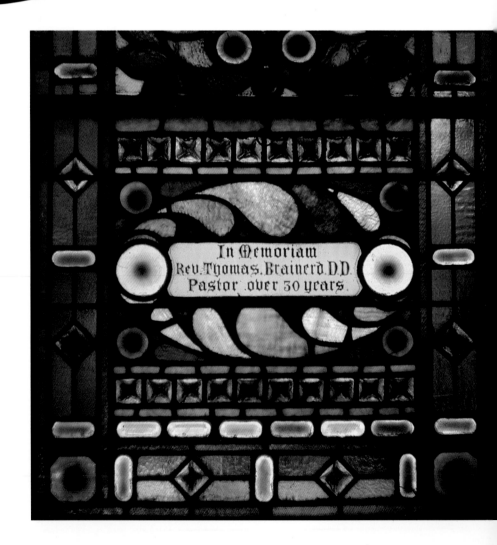

In Memoriam
Rev. Thomas. Brainerd. D.D.
Pastor over 30 years

165, 166. These positive and negative images of an 1890s acid-etched lady are a wistful reminder of the twentieth-century demise of American decorative glass.

was diluted quality, and because church windows were usually large scale and prominently displayed, poor work often became an unfortunate public event.

These years of open discord were a sad decline for American stained glass, and efforts toward intraindustry cooperation led to the formation of the National Ornamental Glass Manufacturers Association, or NOGMA. As remembered by Ludwig Von Gerichten in 1937, there were long-needed improvements in the American stained-glass fraternity:

> ...The older members of our craft will remember the summer of Nineteen Hundred and Three when we met during those hot July days at the Southern Hotel in Columbus, to organize the National Ornamental Glass Manufacturers Association—now known as the Stained Glass Association of America...
>
> ...the reasons which prompted us to form our Association ...[had been that]...the general distintegration of business had been so great at the beginning of the century, that everyone in our craft, was just about discouraged with conditions. Each felt that he could do little alone, in the face of the general apathy then existing.
>
> Labor was well organized, and could concentrate its strength against any individual firm...I recognized Labor's right to organize for its own protection, but it was clearly necessary for our protection to organize the leaders of the craft to ward off strikes and unreasonable demands of labor...
>
> However, the labor situation was by no means the only point of mutual interest. A matter of grave importance was the correction of the ridiculous prices which were being made by so many firms...[5]

If there is any question as to exactly what ills this new group was trying to remedy, NOGMA listed the basic tenets of "What the Association Stands For." Of particular interest are the first four points:

1. To eliminate existing evils.
2. To stop the cutting of prices.
3. To get an equitable price for our product.
4. To have competition conducted honestly.[6]

Despite its problems, the new group had taken three important steps by 1910. First was a campaign to improve international tariff protection, second was the production and distribution of a national catalog of stained-glass designs, and third was the creation of an intraindustry publication known as *The Ornamental Glass Bulletin*.

The tariff question took precedence, very likely because it was a problem on which most American firms could comfortably shed many of their individual and collective woes. As a result, the "good news" was that the campaign eventually did prove successful in achieving increased "economic protection." The bad news, however, was that the question became moot, for only a few artists would have the ability to make their twentieth-century glass art compatible with the rapidly changing taste in architecture.

The second project designed to galvanize American stained-glass producers was the creation. of a national catalog. Quite understandably, it was felt that prices had to become stabilized in order for the ferocious competition to be tamed, and what better way than to provide everyone with the same designs, which could then be confidently sold at nationwide rates? Unfortunately, NOGMA was on the right track but taking the wrong train. Attempting to "standardize" something as creative as stained glass only led to the Gresham's law already mentioned: bad designs drove out the good. Thus NOGMA's book of "high grade, medium class priced" window designs resulted in the wide distribution of mediocre stained-glass ideas as "representative" of the industry's skill. This only reinforced the attitude of both architects and the public that decorative windows were an "old-fashioned" embellishment which could and should be phased out of contemporary architecture.

It is not surprising that the national catalog, for all its big splash of wide distribution, set off few heavy waves of interest. There is little further mention of the project, and most telling, perhaps, is the fact that despite the several thousands of these catalogs which were distributed, almost none has survived.

At this point, it looked like the NOGMA was two strikes down. Fortunately, their third swing proved to be a solid hit, a real game winner, in fact. This was the creation of the magazine first called *The Monthly Visitor*, and then quickly changed to *The Ornamental Glass Bulletin*. Known within the trade as the *Bulletin*, it provided the catalyst which had been missing: a vehicle and forum for sharing stained-glass ideas and opinions. Now, at last, everyone could express his opinion, and even in the rough times of the 1930s and 1940s, it was the *Bulletin* that kept the heart of American stained glass alive and ticking.

Not surprisingly, the establishment of the *Bulletin* as a significant industry force was no easier than the establishment of the organization itself. In the same article where Von Gerichten related the events which led to the formation of the NOGMA, he also told of the trials of getting the magazine off the ground:

> Within a year after the founding of the Association we felt the need of some periodical communication between our members as a means of sustaining mutual understanding, and while I was still Secretary, we started a monthly paper which was largely supported by the advertising of our friends who supplied us with glass, lead and the other materials of our craft.
>
> As Editor my continual effort was to keep every member aware of the fact that he was part of a widespread national group with common interests and problems.

Art Glass in the Home

THE staining of glass and leading it into intricate and pleasing designs was one of the earliest mediums for the expression of art. It reached its height early in the sixteenth century when a satisfactory process of coloring glass was discovered. Prior to this the colored effect was attained by painting the glass. One needs only to visit the historic chapels and cathedrals of Europe to realize the wonderful effects which can be attained with colored glass. There is scarcely a home which does not have some window or door which would be rendered much more attractive by the use of well chosen stained glass. It is well to bear in mind that the most pleasing effects will be obtained if the colored glass is placed on the light side of a room where there is the least amount of light thrown on it from the inside. And remember that the making of harmonious designs is a craft, a science and an art. We leave it to your judgment whether or not the following Morgan designs bear the stamp of artistry.

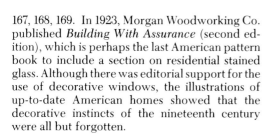

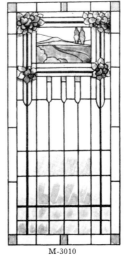

M-3010

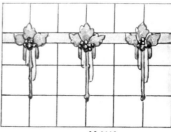

M-3013

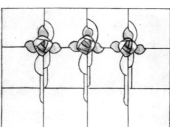

M-3014

M-3011

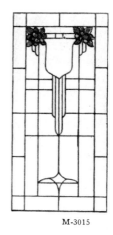

M-3015

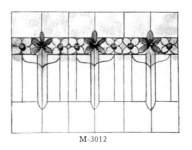

M-3012

These Morgan Designs made in all sizes.

167, 168, 169. In 1923, Morgan Woodworking Co. published *Building With Assurance* (second edition), which is perhaps the last American pattern book to include a section on residential stained glass. Although there was editorial support for the use of decorative windows, the illustrations of up-to-date American homes showed that the decorative instincts of the nineteenth century were all but forgotten.

We all thought the paper was a good idea, but the main difficulty was to get contributions of news and articles from the members. There were many kind promises, but no copy from anyone for months.

But I finally hit upon a ruse to draw the fire from my dear fellow members. I wrote a scathing reply to one of my own articles, and printed it under an assumed name.

In the next issue I answered that in detail, admitting the truth of some of the arguments brought forth, but stoutly maintaining other points in my first article.

Even this did not at first bring results, so I increased my

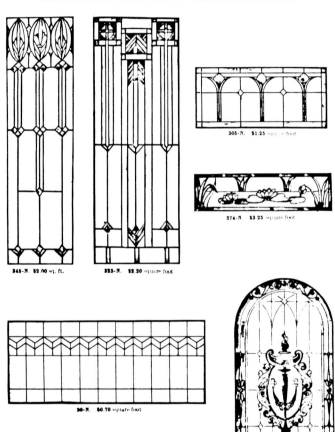

170. Members of the National Ornamental Glass Manufacturers Association, such as the Chicago firm of Flanagan & Biedenweg, could sign up for personalized copies of the *Official Catalogue* of 1909. However, the public was losing interest in art glass, and these examples show that there was little originality left in decorative-window design.

opposition the following month all under different names, and that did the trick!

Everyone watched for the paper each month, eager to follow the controversy and to contribute their own point of view. I rarely had to write a "fill-in" and the magazine was on its way.[7]

One of those articles written by Von Gerichten in 1909 discussed price cutting, and indicates that no matter what the tariff situation, nor how "adequate" a catalog was created, American stained glass at the turn of the century had a serious problem with interstudio rivalries:

When Do We Reach Bottom?

This is a question that has been asked by many a stained glass firm within the last six or seven years, very frequently. Prices have been going lower and lower in spite of the fact that labor is considerably higher than it ever was before...

...the presumption of several years ago that we had reached the bottom on prices, which looked absolutely to be the fact, has been upset by later developments of prices going still lower...

...We have been trying as a national organization to improve conditions, but it seems the personal jealousies of individual members blinds them to such a degree that they cannot see anybody else getting the job away from them...[8]

Many other letters echoed this opinion, and in 1916 the problem was still apparent, as discussed by a fellow from Ohio, who asked, "What ails the stained glass industry?":

Why is it that men engaged in other lines become successful financially, while those engaged in the manufacture of stained glass windows are as a rule poorer after a long and hard struggle than they were when they started out, full of hope and confidence?

...It is enough to say that if one-tenth of the time which was wasted in wrangling and mud-slinging would be utilized in getting together for the good of the industry as a whole, it could be turned from a mediocre and half-hearted affair into one of the most successful industries in the United States.

(Signed) F. M. Hayes
with
Dayton Glassworks
Dayton, Ohio[9]

One year later, the U.S. Department of Commerce did a study of the cost of glass in the United States, which substantiated the comments of the stained-glass producers themselves:

...Not only have American glass manufacturers had to meet sharp foreign competition in several lines, but there is probably no industry that has suffered more from intensive

171. Only in America could stained glass and hamburgers be combined, c. 1930.

competition among domestic manufacturers… Hand manufacturers have struggled desperately against the competition of those using machines and often the market was demoralized in consequence. Ruinous competition is usually the result of trying to fix prices without a knowledge of the unit costs of production.

A large proportion of the establishments that were visited during this investigation had crude cost-finding methods and poor general accounting systems…[10]

But is it logical to expect artists to be businesslike, or entrepreneurs to be artistic? Mr. Hayes had also asked if stained glassmen "…are…businessmen with a working knowledge of art, or…artists without a working knowledge of business?" Of course, the answer is as complex as the question, for if a stained-glass designer declared himself an "artist," then his efforts toward making a good living required asking for too personal a commitment from his clients. If he declared that he was really a businessman, then his best works were relegated to the ranks of "commercial products," and therefore subjected to the harsh realities of catalog prices, cutthroat bidding, and irrational supply and demand. Either way, the serious stained-glass artist was caught in a squeeze play and the result was the steady reduction of decorative window art.

Even if the economic problems had been solved, however, there was still the specter of the opalescent flummydiddle, which continued to chafe at the stained-glass traditionalists. A typical verbal exchange was printed in the *Bulletin* in 1916, where a sarcastic Englishman gave his opinion of American opalescent creativity:

…To my mind, the opalescent flummydiddle [window] was exceedingly pretty and at the same time a blasphemy against all the sane artistic standards old or new. It was in vile taste, it bespoke humbug, folly, and a denial of the faultless definition which says that, "Art is the expression of man's joy in his work."

…Oh, well, there are bumkins who admire pictures made of postage stamps, and there are cockneys who applaud a violinist for imitating bird calls, while plenty of nice little children will clap their hands if you play a tune on tumblers. Me thinks the attempt to evolve a "regular picture out of glass" is quite as dignified.

…Come, come! Let us keep things separate. East is East and West is West. Pigs is pigs, canvas is canvas, glass is glass…[11]

To the credit of the American side, there appeared a staunch rebuttal in the following month's *Bulletin:*

…The cleverly written word picture in the September Bulletin insults the intelligence of the profession, endeavors to make a joke of La Farge, Tiffany and all the other American artists who decided to break away from the beaten path in art windowmaking, and slaps in the face of the six American glass manufacturers, who have devoted

time, money and talent in developing opalescent glass, and who by their advertising and other aid, helped the Bulletin to its present standing. The boosters of painted antique glass may go the limit of their genius in advancing their cause in their own publication, but it is not right to permit them to villify at the expense of the Bulletin, those progressives who do not believe in resuscitating designs of the Middle Ages to adorn modern buildings.[12]

Unfortunately, the words of this American writer were lost in the turmoil of the next few years. World events suddenly took precedence over national stylistic concerns, and when the troops returned from "over there," the nineteenth century was only a memory. For American decorative windows, the formal end came in 1925, when the June issue of *The Ornamental Glass Bulletin* was published "…in the interest of the National Ornamental Glass Manufacturers Ass'n of the United States and Canada…" and then the July issue appeared as *The Stained Glass Bulletin,* which would henceforth be published "…in the interest of the Stained Glass Association of America."[13] This dramatic change was mentioned only briefly, but in retrospect, it had been a long time coming. Mid-twentieth-century America would thereafter have few good thoughts about our ancestors with the decorative persuasions, and only an occasional ripple of sorrow would surface, such as when the son of John La Farge addressed the SGAA convention in 1944 and said:

When I speak of my father's work in stained glass…I voice a certain resentment…which rests on the idea that my father's work in stained glass took him away from…other finer lines of work…which would not have made the same drain on his physical and nervous energy.

…My father himself was not unaware of the fact that stained glass had exacted a heavy toll upon his own personality…

…was [his] glass worth the price he paid for it in sweat, in labor, in anxiety, and even in illness—indeed over a whole lifetime…All I can say is that it was the price paid by a pioneer…

It is for that reason that although stained glass was…a joy and immense satisfaction to the higher part of his being…it was [the] crucifixion of his flesh…[14]

Hearing these sad words, we wonder how someone with the great talent of La Farge could have his most personal creations rejected; yet it is apparent that this is but one part of the twentieth-century obloquy against the whole versatile display of America's nineteenth-century architectural glass.

Time, fortunately, has proven the weakness of this position, and a serious appraisal of the American contribution to this most magical of artistic mediums now makes it clear that this country's antique, decorative windows stand out as separate, significant, and successful.

172. An American decorative window created by John La Farge in the 1880s. Great glass; significant art.

NOTES

Chapter One

1. Survey to define the term *stained glass*, by the Stained Glass Association of America, *Stained Glass* (Autumn 1962), p. 21

2. Edward Hazen, *The Panorama or Professions and Trades or Every Man's Book* (Philadelphia: Uriah Hunt, 1837, p. vii; reprint, Watkins Glen, N.Y.: The American Life Foundation Study Institute, 1970).

3. *Ibid,* p. 215.

4. *Ibid.*

5. *Ibid,* p. 217.

6. *Ibid.*

7. *Ibid.*

8. H. Hudson Holly, *Modern Dwellings in Town and Country* (New York: Harper & Brothers, 1878, pp. 66, 67; reprint, Watkins Glen, N.Y.: The American Life Foundation, n.d.).

Chapter Two

1. Alan Gowans, *Images of American Living* (Philadelphia: J.B. Lippincott, 1964), p. 282.

2. John Gilbert Lloyd, *Stained Glass in America* (Jenkintown, Pa.: Foundation Books, 1963), p. 44.

3. Gowans, *Images of American Living,* p. 304.

4. Lloyd, *Stained Glass in America,* p. 44.

5. Arthur Channing Downs, Jr., "Stained Glass in American Architecture," *Nineteenth Century* (Winter 1977), 56.

6. Wayne Andrews, *American Gothic* (New York: Random House, 1975), p. 23.

7. Gowans, *Images of American Living,* p. 306.

8. James Marston Fitch, *American Building 1: The Historical Forces That Shaped It* (New York: Schocken Books, 1973), p. 127.

9. Gowans, *Images of American Living,* p. 306.

10. See *Furniture for the Victorian Home* (Watkins Glen, N.Y.: The American Life Foundation Study Institute, 1978; abridged reprint of A. J. Downing, *The Architecture of Country Houses,*

1850, and J. C. Louden, *An Encyclopedia of Cottage, Farm, and Villa Architecture,* 1833).

11. Hazen, *The Panorama or Professions and Trades,* pp. 198–204.

12. *Ibid.*

13. Downs, "Stained Glass in American Architecture," 56.

14. *Ibid.,* p. 58.

15. Downing, *Country Houses* (reprint), p. 19.

16. *Ibid.,* p. 26.

17. *Ibid.,* pp. 88, 89.

18. *Ibid.,* p. 70.

19. *Ibid.,* pp. 72 and 75 (Downing), and pp. 117 and 196 (Louden).

20. Oliver P. Smith, *The Domestic Architect* (Buffalo, N.Y.: Phinney & Co., 1854, p. iii; reprint, *Victorian Domestic Architect* [Watkins Glen, N.Y.: The American Life Foundation Library of Victorian Culture, 1978]).

21. *Ibid.,* p. 23.

22. *Ibid.,* p. 93.

Chapter Three

1. Henry Hudson Holly, *Holly's Country Seats* (New York: D. Appleton & Company, 1863, preface; reprint, Watkins Glen, N.Y.: The American Life Foundation, n.d.).

2. *Ibid.,* p. 111.

3. Geo. E. Woodward, *Architecture and Rural Art No. I* (New York, Geo. E. Woodward, 1868, p. v; reprint, Watkins Glen, N.Y.: The American Life Foundation Library of Victorian Culture, 1978, as *Woodward's Victorian Architecture and Rural Art*).

4. *Ibid.,* p. 57.

5. A. J. Bicknell, *Village Builder and Supplement* (New York: A.J. Bicknell & Co., 1872; reprint, *Victorian Village Builder*[Watkins Glen, N.Y.: The American Life Foundation Study Institute, 1976]).

6. *Ibid.,* title page.

7. *Ibid.*, see the "New Introduction & Commentary" by Paul Goeldner, and plate 6.

8. *Ibid.*, plate 2.

9. A. J. Bicknell, *Detail, Cottage and Constructive Architecture* (New York: A.J. Bicknell & Co, 1873; reprint, Watkins Glen, N.Y.: American Life Foundation, 1975, as *Victorian Architecture*).

10. Christopher Dresser, *Principles of Decorative Design* (London: Cassell, Petter & Galpin, 1875), p. 3.

11. *Ibid.*, p. 153.

12. *Ibid.*, pp. 155–156.

13. *Ibid.*, p. 157.

14. Quoted in Carol Olwell and Judith Lynch Waldhorn, *A Gift to the Street* (San Francisco: Antelope Island Press, 1976), pp. 167–168.

15. Bruce J. Talbert, *Gothic Forms Applied to Furniture Metal Work and Decoration for Domestic Purposes* (Boston: James R. Osgood & Co., 1823); and *Examples of Ancient and Modern Furniture Metal Work Tapestries Decoration Etc.* 2 vols. (Boston: James R. Osgood & Co., 1877; reprint, *Victorian Decorative Arts* [Watkins Glen, N.Y.: The American Life Foundation, 1978]).

16. *Ibid.*, p. 5.

17. *Ibid.*

18. Cox & Sons, *Illustrated Catalogue of Designs for Stained Glass Windows* (London: Cox & Sons, 1876).

19. Charles Booth, *Memorial Stained Glass Windows* (Orange, N.J.: Charles Booth, 1876), p. 19.

20. *Ibid.*, p. 20.

21. George Palliser, *Model Homes for the People* (Bridgeport, Conn., 1876; reprint, Watkins Glen, N.Y.: American Life Foundation, 1978), p. 38.

22. *Model Homes* (Bridgeport, Conn.: Palliser, Palliser, & Co., 1878; reprint, Watkins Glen, N.Y.: The American Life Foundation Library of Victorian Culture, n.d.).

23. *Ibid.*, p. 8.

24. *Ibid.*, p. 30.

25. *Ibid.*

26. *Ibid.*, p. 44.

27. H. Hudson Holly, *Modern Dwellings in Town and Country* (New York: Harper & Brothers, 1878, preface; reprint, Watkins Glen, N.Y.: The American Life Foundation, n.d.).

28. *Ibid.*, p. 82.

29. *Ibid.*, p. 17.

30. *Ibid.*, pp. 66–69.

31. *Ibid.*, p. 150, compare with Cox & Sons *Illustrated Catalogue*, p. 27.

32. *Specimen Book of One Hundred Architectural Designs* (New York: Bicknell & Comstock, 1880; reprint, Watkins Glen, N.Y.: The American Life Foundation Study Institute, n.d.), p. 71.

33. *Modern Architectural Designs and Details* (New York: William T. Comstock, 1881), preface; reprint, *Victorian Architecture* [Watkins Glen, N.Y.: American Life Foundation, 1975]).

34. *New Cottage Homes and Details* (New York: Palliser, Palliser, & Co., 1887, introduction; reprint, Watkins Glen, N.Y.: The American Life Foundation, n.d.).

35. John Calvin Stevens and Albert Winslow Cobb, *Examples of American Domestic Architecture* (New York: William T. Comstock, 1889; reprint, *American Domestic Architecture—A Late Victorian Stylebook* [Watkins Glen, N.Y.: The American Life Foundation Study Institute, 1978], see notes for plate XXXI).

36. *The Ornamental Glass Bulletin* (December 1907), p. 2.

Chapter Four

1. Robert and Gertrude Metcalf, *Making Stained Glass* (Newton Abbott, England: David & Charles, 1972), p. 35.

Chapter Five

1. Palliser, *Model Homes*, p. 70.

2. *Ibid.*

3. *Ibid.*

4. See H. Weber Wilson, "The Controversial History of Residential Stained Glass," *Stained Glass* (Fall 1979), 228–232. Typical modern assessments of Tiffany by traditional artists include the quote from Metcalf and Metcalf, *Making Stained Glass*, and the following from Lawrence Lee, George Seddon, and Francis Stephans *Stained Glass* (New York: Crown Publishers, 1979): "Louis Comfort Tiffany was a man of immensely varied talents who frequently talked and created meretricious rubbish" (p. 156).

5. *Stained Glass* (Winter 1936–1937), 73–78.

6. *The Monthly Visitor* (January 1907), i.

7. *Stained Glass* (Winter 1936–1937), 73–78.

8. *The Ornamental Glass Bulletin* (June 1909), 1–3.

9. *The Ornamental Glass Bulletin* (February 1916), 56.

10. *The Ornamental Glass Bulletin* (November 1917), 7.

11. *The Ornamental Glass Bulletin* (September 1916), 6–10.

12. *The Ornamental Glass Bulletin* (October 1916), 3.

13. At their national convention in June 1925, the National Ornamental Glass Manufacturers Association of America changed their name to the Stained Glass Association of America (SGAA). In July, their monthly magazine appeared as *The Stained Glass Bulletin*. In August 1925, the magazine was titled *The Bulletin of the Stained Glass Association of America*. In 1931, the magazine adopted its present title, *Stained Glass*.

14. *Stained Glass* (Winter 1944), 111.

GLOSSARY

antique glass Colored, mouth-blown sheet glass of the type used in medieval church windows. Such glass (now called *full antique*) continues to be made today. The colors are crisp, and the interior variegations are desirable for their irregular light refraction. Antique glass is traditionally used in the best-quality church windows. In the United States it has been used very selectively in residential work.

arabesque A complex curvilinear pattern found in Renaissance decoration that is often composed of floral and vine motifs. It has antecedents in Islamic architecture.

art glass Usually refers to turn-of-the-century windows made with opalescent glass because the multicolored variegations within the glass could be used to create painterly effects. The term *art glass* was actually in use before opalescent windows became popular.

balloon frame The construction system that uses mill-cut studs, joists, and rafters, all nailed together. When this building system supplanted hand-hewn post-and-beam construction in the 1840s, houses could be built so quickly that it looked as if they were being inflated by an air pump.

balustrade A heavy railing system, often found on exterior rooflines or balconies.

bargeboard Wide, decorative boards attached to the gable end, especially popular on Victorian Gothic Revival houses.

beveled glass Plate glass that has its edges ground and polished to an angle. The nineteenth-century beveling process had four steps: (1) rough grinding on a cast-iron "mill" with sand and water; (2) smoothing on a sandstone wheel; (3) polishing on a wooden wheel with fine pumice; and (4) brilliant polishing on a felt wheel with ferrous oxide. Beveled mosaics were usually set in zinc or brass cames.

bay window A usually curved or three-sided window that projects from the ground floor of a building. Decorative glass is often found in the transoms or upper sash of bay windows.

brilliant-cut glass Another name for wheel-cut or engraved glass. Brilliant-cut window designs are created by moving the glass over vertically rotating stone wheels. Different shapes incise different lines or spots. Roughed-in designs are polished over felt wheels with black rouge.

cames The strips of metal that are used to hold together glass mosaics. Derived from the Greek word for reeds (*kalmus*), which in the Middle Ages were bound together and used as crude forms for casting lead. Cames are found in many shapes and sizes and have been made from lead, zinc, brass, pewter, and German silver.

Carpenter Gothic A style of mid-nineteenth-century American house to which elaborate sawn-wood ornament was applied. The objective was to emulate "authentic" Gothic houses, which were usually laid up in stone.

cartoon The full-scale drawing from which the individual pieces of a stained-glass window are cut. Also used as a guide when the window is leaded up.

carved glass Deeply incised glass. Usually refers to nineteenth-century wheel-cut work or modern sandblasting.

casement window (1) A fixed window that is not meant to be opened; or (2) a glazed sash hinged to a frame, meant to be swung open. Iron casements are often found in masonry construction. Wooden casement windows were used in Pilgrim-century buildings.

cathedral glass Machine-made glass, usually found in pale tints with textural effects. "Streaky" cathedral glass exhibits swirls of various colors, and America's early cathedral glass (c. 1860) had fascinating primitive irregularities. Cathedral glass has no specific relationship to churches.

clapboards Horizontal wooden siding used on both timber-frame and balloon-frame houses. The correct pronunciation is "clab'brd."

Classicism Refers to the presumed "laws" of architecture that were believed to have governed the construction of Greek and Roman buildings. Modern Classical ideals emerged with the Renaissance in southern Europe about 1400, and were influenced too much by the gnomish writings of an obscure Roman named Vitruvius. Since then, "Classical" styles have contrasted sharply, for example, the Baroque, Georgian, and Greek Revival modes. It should be noted that originally the Greeks and Romans painted their buildings in bright colors.

cornice The heavy molding that covers the upper part of a building where the roof and walls meet. This was often embellished with decorative brackets and other ornamentation.

crackle glass Produced by immersing hot glass in water, which causes fissures on the surface. These lacerations often form a pattern that resembles alligator skin.

crocket A plantlike Gothic ornament used to decorate vertical building elements such as spires and gables.

crown glass Early sheet glass made by spinning large, thin circles or "crowns," which were then cut into window panes. At the thick center was the "bull's-eye," which was also saved for cruder glazing. Being mouth-blown and hand-finished, crown glass was optically clear but rather expensive.

dormer An attic-story window that is under its own gable and framed out beyond the roofline. Often found on larger American houses of the eighteenth century. Dormer windows provided light and ventilation for the servants' quarters or "dormitories."

double hung A window composed of an upper and a lower sash set in a frame so that one or both can slide up and down.

drapery The folds of fabric that clothe Classical figures as depicted in art and architecture.

drapery glass Hand-formed sheet glass that resembles Classical drapery. Developed in America in the late nineteenth century, it was used primarily in large, opalescent figural windows.

embossed glass Glass with raised relief decoration. This can be done by pressing a pattern onto the surface or by etching away the background.

enamel paints Bright, multicolored paints that are applied to glass but do not fire well, so that over time, they will often fade or weather off.

engraved glass Another name for wheel-cut or brilliant-cut decoration on glass. The design is incised into the surface of the glass with stone or copper wheels. The incisions of brilliant-cut glass are further enhanced by polishing.

etched glass From the old German *etzen*, "to cause to eat." Nineteenth-century acid etching was done by coating glass with a resistant material such as paraffin, picking out the design with a sharp instrument, and dissolving the exposed areas with hydrofluoric acid. This process was time-consuming and extremely hazardous. A faster, safer method used sandblasting and stencils, which obscured the glass but usually did not cut below the surface.

Federal style The architecture of the early American Republic, c. 1790–1830. There was a continued emphasis on Classical themes but the introduction of oval windows, curved facades, and such patriotic embellishments as pedimented eagles indicated that American architecture would evolve in response to the needs and stimulations of a developing culture.

fenestration The arrangement of window and door openings in a building.

festoon Similar to a garland or swag. A decorative loop that in window designs often appears as a string of jewels; sometimes the ends are tied off with ribbons.

figured glass In pattern books of the mid-nineteenth century this referred to wheel-cut glass. By the turn of the century it also referred to etched and pressed-pattern glass.

fillets Narrow strips of glass used around the border of a mosaic window. In olden times, when stained glass was cemented into masonry openings, the fillets were meant to be broken if the window had to be removed. In the nineteenth century, one of the earliest decorative window styles was the use of wheel-cut fillets around leaded quarries. Such windows were usually glazed into wooden sash, which was then set into the framed opening.

flashed glass Glass made up of a thick base color and a micro-thin "flashed" layer of contrasting color. Red flashed on white (clear glass) is well known, but many other combinations are found, including blue on yellow. When the flashed layer is removed by etching or wheel-cutting, designs of contrasting colors are created.

fleur-de-lis The royal French lily stylized into ornament. This form originated in French Gothic art and architecture and became one of the most popular elements in nineteenth-century American decorative windows.

gable end The wall under the roof gable, especially that portion which encloses the attic story. A popular spot to set fancy mullioned windows.

garland Like a swag or festoon, a decorative loop that usually incorporates floral and fruit motifs, often bound with a ribbon.

Georgian architecture Buildings constructed between the reign of George I (1713) and George III (1830). The dominant theme was Neo-Classicism, with an emphasis on Palladian interpretations.

giant order A Palladian motif in which columns and their bases and capitals were scaled to rise more than one story.

glass stainers' colors The "paints" used by traditional stained-glass artists. These are actually monochromatic vitreous oxides that range in color from "tracing black" to rusty brown. These colors are brushed onto glass, then matted, stippled, picked, shaded, and otherwise worked before being fired in a kiln. The oxides then become permanently fused onto the glass.

glue-chip glass Clear or colored glass that has a frostlike surface. Produced by coating glass with animal-hide glue that is heated and then shrinks, taking off slivers of glass.

jewel Smooth, faceted, pressed, or chipped pieces of glass usually made to imitate precious stones. Prolific use of these decorative inserts is a hallmark of American windows of the 1880s and 1890s. The jewels were made in all shapes and sizes, were frequently set in clusters or strung out as festoons, and were occasionally cast in figural forms.

lace glass Delicate patterns sandblasted on glass. Often found in entrance areas and kitchen-cupboard doors.

leaded glass Specifically, pieces of glass held together in a web of lead cames. Generally refers to very simple mosaic patterns glazed only with clear glass.

light An opening in a structure through which daylight can enter. Can also refer to a specific window or window fill, such as "leaded light."

medallion window A decorative window, usually of leaded glass, in the center of which is a circular panel on which a figure, scene, or significant symbol has been painted.

milk glass Milky-white glass with opaline characteristics such as bluish tinges and a fiery red inner glow. Developed in the mid-nineteenth century, it was very popular for parlor and dressing-room vessels. The precursor of opalescent glass: it is said that sunlight illuminating a milk-glass dish inspired John La Farge to create opalescent glass.

mosaic construction Decorative windows comprising many pieces of glass, each cut separately, and usually held together within a network of metal cames. Can refer to leaded glass, beveled glass, mercury mosaics, and complex designs set in wooden mullions.

mullion Specifically, the heavy, vertical supporting member that separates the openings of a multilight window. Often made of masonry and well defined in traceried lights. Generally, however, "mullion" has come to mean the thin wood moldings (both horizontal and vertical) that separate the glass in a multipaned sash.

muntin A vertical member that separates the panels in a door. Also, the vertical molding that separates the glass in a multipaned light.

Neo-Classicism The several periods when architecture

tried to reestablish "pure" Greek and Roman forms. It is always tempered by a reflection of current taste as well as historical dogma.

opalescent glass   Glass with opaque, variegated colors, in which light is held and refracted internally. Also referred to as "art glass" and "American glass." Considered the antithesis of antique glass (pot metal), it was denounced by traditional religious window artists. Produced and used primarily in America, it is found in both secular and ecclesiastical buildings.

oriel window   A window that projects from an upper-story facade. Usually three-sided, and in the late nineteenth century used widely in urban rowhouse design. Oriel windows often extend more than one story and frequently feature stained or beveled glass in the upper sash or transoms.

painted glass   Windows that have been decorated with either monochromatic oxides (glass stainers' colors) or with colored enamel paints. Such a window could be of mosaic construction or a single pane.

paisley   A teardrop-shaped design in which a curving line folds back upon itself. One of the hallmark motifs of Renaissance-style stained glass. Also frequently found in fancy beveled glass.

Palladian window   Also called a "Venetian" window or "Serlian motif" because it first appeared in Serlio's *Architettura* in 1537. It is a three-light opening with a roundheaded center section flanked by squareheaded sidelights. This form was widely used by Palladio, but never as a window; that adaptation emerged out of English Palladianism in the mid-1700s. Traditional Palladian windows occur frequently in American eighteenth-century buildings. In the late nineteenth century this window form was reworked in many variations, often including glazing with colored glass. It can be found in all manner of variations and often includes decorative glazing.

Palladio, Andrea (1508–1580)   Italian Renaissance architect whose ideas had a profound effect on Classical building throughout Europe. Palladio stressed harmonious proportions, symmetrical planning, and natural settings. English Palladianism did not emerge until the early 1700s, and shortly thereafter American Colonial architecture was also greatly affected. Popular Palladian motifs were pavilion fronts, supported with multistory columns and pilasters and service wings extending away from the main building. This enlarged entrance area set up the space and rationale for incorporating decorative windows around the main entrance. The Palladian influence also set up the space for a major window above the entrance or at the second-story rear, which generally illuminated the main staircase landing.

pediment   Strictly speaking, the triangular end of a building above the cornice, as seen on a "temple front." Also used to describe the heavy molding set above windows and doors, which is usually triangular, sometimes with curved sides, and sometimes with a "broken arch" or "broken top."

pilaster   A nonstructural column or pillar that protrudes only slightly from a wall and usually comprises a base, shaft, and capital. Often used to unify the series of columns under a porch or portico. Also found on fireplace mantels, architectural furniture, and interior entrances.

plate glass   Machine-made glass that has been ground and polished so that it is free from flaws and distortions. It is usually at least ¼″ thick and is used primarily for bevels, mirrors, and large store windows. Until the early twentieth century, polished plate was optically much clearer than standard window glass.

portico   A projecting roof supported by columns, usually found at the main entrance to a building.

pot metal   Another term for full-antique (mouth-blown) colored glass.

pressed-pattern glass   Machine-rolled sheet glass with one surface embossed with an overall pattern. Usually found in white (clear glass) but also seen in several pale tones. Dozens of patterns were available around the turn of the century. Many fine windows were composed of several contrasting patterns leaded into intricate mosaics.

punty   The iron rod used to dip a molten "gather" of glass out of the melting pot.

quarry   Glass cut into the shape of a diamond or square. Quarried windows have such pieces leaded up with vertical points, with the cames thus running on the diagonal. Same as "quarrel."

Queen Anne sash   A window sash in which wooden mullions form rectangular patterns, usually a field of small squares or a series of squares surrounding a larger central rectangle. Usually glazed with panes of clear, cathedral, or flashed glass. Sometimes individual mosaic panels or other special decoration were glazed in symmetrical spaces. Not necessarily the predominant window fill of the American Queen Anne house.

rosette A small ornament cast in lead and used to cover the solder joint where several cames converge. Used often in the Georgian and Federal periods, and later, in nineteenth-century Neo-Classical buildings.

roundheaded A window or door that forms an arched opening. Traditionally used for the center light of a Palladian window.

sash Wood or metal framing that holds the window glass. Double-hung sash slides up and down. Casement sash is framed in permanently or hinged to swing open.

sawn-wood ornament An architectural embellishment cut from wood, often intended to appear to be made of stone. Such decoration is typical of both Carpenter Gothic and Queen Anne "gingerbread" houses.

silver stain The clear solution of silver nitrate that is applied to glass on the opposite side from any painted detail. It is usually fired separately and turns various shades of yellow. This phenomenon is the basis for the term "stained glass."

solder A mixture of tin and lead, which for glass workers is manufactured to melt around 400° F. After leading up, all the cames of a mosaic window are joined with a thin layer of solder.

squareheaded A door or window opening that is rectangular.

stained glass Traditionally, leaded mosaic windows of colored glass that have also been painted and fired, with or without the additional application of silver stain. The term has come to represent any mosaic window, with or without paint or stain, composed of glass that is colored or clear.

support bars Iron bars that are fastened to the inside of mosaic window and door panels to help support the weight of the glass and the metal cames.

swag A festoon, usually of cloth or drapery, sometimes including fruits and flowers.

temple front A building that has the main entrance at the gable end. Typical of Greek Revival architecture.

terra-cotta Unglazed, fired clay used extensively in late nineteenth-century American building. It is found in reds and yellows and was often sculpted into ornate figures and patterns.

tessera A small piece of marble, glass, or stone used in making traditional mosaics.

transitional window A decorative window in which the design incorporates motifs from a currently popular style and also elements from an incoming fashion. Often seen when flamboyant Renaissance window designs began to moderate into the more conservative Neo-Classical mode.

transom The horizontal cross-member above a door or window opening. Also refers to the actual window that is placed in the transom area.

volute A spiral or whorl such as may be found on Ionic and Corinthian capitals. This shape was popular with nineteenth-century American glass artists who often terminated their scrolling leadlines with a jewel.

wheel-cut glass Incised decoration produced with either copper or stone wheels. Wheel-cut glassware was usually left with a dull, matte finish. In the nineteenth century wheel-cut doors and windows received a second, brilliant polishing. See *brilliant-cut glass*.

"Wrenaissance" Refers to the architecture of Sir Christopher Wren (1632–1723) who was responsible for rebuilding London after the great fire of 1666. His ideas infused a Neo-Classical (Renaissance) spirit into English architecture, which was shortly transferred to the British Colonies in North America.

BIBLIOGRAPHY

Books About Nineteenth-Century Culture and Architectural Design

Andrews, Wayne. *American Gothic*. New York: Random House, 1975.

Barnard, Julian. *The Decorative Tradition*. Princeton, N.J.: The Pyne Press, 1973.

Dresser, Christopher. *Principles of Decorative Design*. London: Cassell, Petter & Galpin, 1875.

Fitch, James Marsden. *American Building 1: The Historical Forces That Shaped It*. New York: Schocken Books, 1973.

Furniture for the Victorian Home. Watkins Glen, N.Y.: The American Life Foundation Study Institute, 1978. Abridged reprint of A. J. Downing, *The Architecture of Country Houses; Including Designs for Cottages, Farm Houses, and the Best Modes of Warming and Ventilating*. United States, 1850; and J. C. Louden, *An Encyclopedia of Cottage, Farm, and Villa Architecture*. Great Britain, 1830.

Gillon, Edmund B. *Early Illustrations and Views of American Architecture*. New York: Dover Publications, 1971.

Gowans, Alan. *Images of American Living*. Philadelphia: J. B. Lippincott, 1964.

Hazen, Edward. *The Panorama or Professions and Trades or Every Man's Book*. Philadelphia: Uriah Hunt, 1837. Reprint. *Edward Hazen's Panorama of Victorian Trades & Professions*. Watkins Glen, N.Y.: The American Life Foundation Study Institute, 1970.

Kidney, Walter C. *The Architecture of Choice: Eclecticism in America 1880 to 1930*. New York: George Braziller, 1974.

Maass, John. *The Glorious Enterprise*. Watkins Glen, N.Y.: American Life Foundation, 1973.

Pierson, William H., Jr. *American Buildings and Their Architects: The Colonial and NeoClassical Styles*. Garden City, N.Y.: Doubleday & Co., 1970.

_____. *American Buildings and Their Architects: Technology and the Picturesque, The Corporate and the Early Gothic Styles*. Garden City, N.Y.: Anchor Press/Doubleday, 1980.

Pitts, Carolyn; Fish, Michael; McCauley, Hugh J.; and Baux, Trina. *The Cape May Handbook*. Philadelphia: Atheneum, 1977.

Roth, Leland M. *A Concise History of American Architecture*. New York: Harper & Row, 1979.

Talbert, Bruce J. *Gothic Forms Applied to Furniture Metal Work and Decoration for Domestic Purposes*. Boston: James R. Osgood & Co., 1873 and *Examples of Ancient and Modern Furniture Metal Work Tapestries Decorations Etc*. 2 vols. Boston: James R. Osgood & Co., 1877. Reprint. *Victorian Decorative Arts*. Watkins Glen, N.Y.: The American Life Foundation, 1978.

Waldhorn, Judith Lynch, and Olwell, Carole. *A Gift to the Street*. San Francisco: Antelope Island Press, 1976.

Whiffen, Marcus. *American Architecture Since 1700: A Guide to the Styles*. Cambridge, Mass.: The M.I.T. Press, 1969.

Books and Articles About Stained-Glass History and Glassworking Techniques

Armitage, E. Liddall. *Stained Glass—History, Technology and Practice*. London: Leonard Hill, 1959.

Blachford, G., and Divine, J. A. F. *Stained Glass Craft*. London and New York: Frederick Warne, 1940.

Booth, Charles. *Memorial Stained Glass Windows*. Orange, N.J.: Charles Booth, 1876.

Cook, F. Palmer. *Talk to Me of Windows*. New York: A. S. Barnes, 1970.

Cooper, William. *The Crown Glass Cutter and Glazier's Manual*. Edinburgh, Scotland: Oliver and Boyd, 1835.

Cox & Sons. *Illustrated Catalogue of Designs for Stained Glass Windows*. London: Cox & Sons, 1876.

French, Jennie. *Glass-Works The Copper Foil Technique of Stained Glass*. New York: Van Nostrand Reinhold Company, 1974.

Glass: History, Manufacture and Its Universal Application. Pittsburgh: Pittsburgh Plate Glass Company, 1923.

Koch, Robert. *Louis C. Tiffany, Rebel in Glass*. New York: Crown Publishers, 1964.

———. *Louis C. Tiffany's Glass, Bronzes, and Lamps: A Complete Collector's Guide*. New York: Crown Publishers, 1971.

Lauber, Joseph. "European Versus American Color Windows." *The Architectural Record* (February 1912), 138–151.

"The Leading and Glass Painting Industry." *Scientific American* (November 24, 1894), 331.

Lee, Lawrence; Seddon, George; and Stephans, Francis. *Stained Glass*. New York: Crown Publishers, 1979.

Lloyd, John Gilbert. *Stained Glass in America*. Jenkintown, Pa.: Foundation Books, 1963.

Metcalf, Robert, and Metcalf, Gertrude. *Making Stained Glass*. Newton Abbott, England: David & Charles, 1972.

Mollica, Peter. *Stained Glass Primer*. vol. 2. Berkeley, Calif.: Mollica Stained Glass Press, 1977.

Powell, Edith Hopps. *San Francisco's Heritage in Art Glass*. Seattle: Salisbury Press, 1976.

Rigan, Otto B. *New Glass*. New York: Ballantine Books, 1976.

Snell, Henry James. *Practical Instructions in Enamel Painting on Glass, China, Tiles, etc., to Which is Added Full Instructions for the Manufacture of the Vitrious Pigments Required with 12 Pages of Illustrations*. London: Brody and Middleton, also Simpkin, Marshall, date unknown (19th century).

"Stained Glass and Objects of Wirecloth." *Scientific American* (May 31, 1890), 347.

"The Stained Glass Window Industry." *Scientific American* (June 1, 1895), 345.

"Stained Glass Windows" (Letter to the Editor). *The Nation* (December 8, 1892), 431.

Whall, C. W. *Stained Glass Work*. The Artistic Crafts Series of Technical Hand Books. London: Sir Isaac Pitman and Sons, 1931.

Wilson, H. Weber. "The Controversial History of Residential Stained Glass." *Stained Glass* (Fall 1979), 228–232.

———. "Etched and Brilliant Cut Glass." *The Old House Journal* (July 1978), 77–78.

———. "Fancy Beveled Glass." *The Old House Journal* (November 1978), 123–124.

———. *Field Guide to American Residential Stained Glass*. Chambersburg, Pa.: Architectural Ecology, 1979.

———. "How to Revive the Splendor of Your Stained Glass." *Historic Preservation* (May/June 1979), 12–16.

———. "Window Glass." *The Old House Journal* (April 1978), 37, 42–45.

———. *Your Residential Stained Glass—A Practical Guide to Repair & Maintenance*. Chambersburg, Pa.: Architectural Ecology, 1979.

Architectural Pattern Books and Other Illustrative Publications

Architectural Interior and Exterior Woodwork Standardized: The Permanent Furniture for Your Home. Clinton, Iowa: The Curtis Company, 1920.

Bicknell, A. J. *Village Builder and Supplement*. New York: A.J. Bicknell & Co., 1872. Reprint. *Victorian Village Builder*. Watkins Glen, N.Y.: American Life Foundation & Study Institute, 1976.

Building with Assurance. Oshkosh, Wis.: The Morgan Woodwork Organization, 1923.

Combined Book of Sash, Doors, Blinds, Moldings, Airwork, Mantels Glass Lists, etc., Including Latest Styles, Elevations, Designs, etc. of Embossed Ground and Cut Glass. Pittsburgh and Read City, Mich.: Schuette and Company, 1892 and 1893.

Holly, Henry Hudson. *Holly's Country Seats*. New York: D. Appleton and Company, 1863. Reprint. Watkins Glen, N.Y.: The American Life Foundation, n.d.

———. *Modern Dwellings in Town and Country*. New York: Harper & Brothers, 1878. Reprint. Watkins Glen, N.Y.: The American Life Foundation, n.d.

Hussey, E. C. *Victorian Home Building, A Trans-Continental View*. Reprint. Watkins Glen, N.Y.: The American Life Foundation, 1976.

Model Homes. Bridgeport, Conn.: Palliser, Palliser and Company, 1878. Reprint. Watkins Glen, N.Y.: American Life Foundation, n.d.

New Cottage Homes and Details. New York: Palliser, Palliser and Company, 1887. Reprint. Watkins Glen, N.Y.: American Life Foundation, n.d.

Palliser, Geo. *Model Homes*. Bridgeport, Conn.: George Palliser, 1876.

———. *Model Homes for the People*. Bridgeport, Conn.: George Palliser, 1876. Reprint. *George Palliser's Model Homes for the People*. Watkins Glen, N.Y.: American Life Foundation, 1978.

Smith, Oliver P. *The Domestic Architect*. New York: Ivison and Phinney, 1854. Reprint. Watkins Glen, N.Y.: American Life Foundation, 1978.

The Stained Glass Windows of St. Joseph. St. Joseph, Mo.: Albrecht Art Museum, 1976.

Stevens, John Calvin, and Cobb, Albert Winslow. *Examples of American Domestic Architecture*. New York: William T. Comstock, 1889. Reprint. *American Domestic Architecture— A Late Victorian Stylebook*. Watkins Glen, N.Y.: The American Life Foundation & Study Institute, 1978.

Victorian Architectural Details. Watkins Glen, N.Y.: The American Life Foundation & Study Institute, 1978. Reprint comprises: Cummings, M. F., and Miller, C. C. *Architecture: Designs for Street Fronts, Suburban Houses, and Cottages*. Toledo, O.: S. Bailey & Eager, 1868; and Cummings, M. F. *Architectural Details*. New York: Orange Judd & Co., 1873.

Victorian Architecture. Watkins Glen, N.Y.: American Life Foundation, 1975. Reprint comprises: *Detail, Cottage and Constructive Architecture*. New York: A.J. Bicknell & Co., 1873; and *Modern Architectural Designs and Details*. New York: William T. Comstock, 1881.

Village Builder and Supplement. New York: A. J. Bicknell & Co., 1872. Reprint. Watkins Glen, N.Y.: The American Life Foundation, 1976.

Woodward, George E. *Architecture and Rural Art*. New York: Geo. E. Woodward, 1867 (vol. 1) and 1868 (vol. 2). Reprint. *Woodward's Victorian Architecture and Rural Art*. Watkins Glen, N.Y.: The American Life Foundation, 1978.

INDEX